AN EIGHTEENTH-CENTURY
INDUSTRIALIST

THE FILE WORKS ERECTED BY PETER STUBS, 1802

AN
EIGHTEENTH-CENTURY INDUSTRIALIST

PETER STUBS OF WARRINGTON
1756–1806

BY

T. S. ASHTON

MANCHESTER UNIVERSITY PRESS

08441423

$L000058130$

Published by the University of Manchester at
THE UNIVERSITY PRESS
316-324, Oxford Road, Manchester 13

FIRST PUBLISHED IN 1939
REPRINTED 1961

CONTENTS

ILLUSTRATIONS

PREFACE

BUSINESS history, as distinct from economic history, is a new field of study : its boundaries have yet to be set and its function defined. But already enough has been done to show that, just as microscopic work on cells may throw new light on the human body, so detailed study of the growth of particular business units may add to knowledge of the industrial system. It is in the hope of helping economic historians to establish more surely their generalizations that books of this kind are written.

It was, I think, in the autumn of 1923 that Mr. F. Aylmer Frost, head of the firm of Peter Stubs Ltd., told Professor Daniels that there was a mass of old letters and account books in the loft of one of the buildings of the concern in Warrington. Professor Unwin, who had just completed his illuminating biography of Samuel Oldknow, on the basis of a similar series of business records, at once set out with Daniels to survey the find. They returned with samples ; and the sight of Unwin, a bundle of records in one hand and a hearth-brush in the other, his face grimed but shining with excitement, is a permanent memory. Shortly afterwards I went with Daniels to Warrington to arrange for the transfer of the documents to the University ; and (perhaps because I was supposed to have some little knowledge of the early metal trades) Daniels and Unwin generously handed over the material to me, with injunctions to make from it a volume that might serve as companion to *Samuel Oldknow and the Arkwrights*. In this I cannot hope to have succeeded ; but at least the attempt has now been made. It is a matter of reproach that other tasks were allowed precedence and that the book was not completed in time for either Unwin or Daniels to see it.

To Mr. F. Aylmer Frost I owe deep gratitude, not only for his gift of the records to the University, but also for information, given in many conversations, about his great-grandfather, Peter Stubs. Two other Directors of the firm, Mr. E. Surrey Dane and Mr. H. R. Milling, have helped in many ways, and without their generous support the book might never have been published : in particular, Mr. Dane helped me to trace several documents and provided the photographs of the original buildings from which the frontispiece has been made.

Professor G. S. Veitch of Liverpool has placed at my disposal his unrivalled knowledge of local history ; Professor D. S. Torrens of Trinity College, Dublin, has provided a great deal of technical information and has read through the proofs ; and Mr. Robert Ward, a student in an extra-mural class I conducted in Sheffield in 1912–13, and a lifelong friend, has taught me much about the file trade to which he was apprenticed nearly fifty years ago. Warm thanks are also due to Mr. Reginald Edge, of the department of Architecture at Manchester, for his drawing of the file works, to Mr. Gordon Bennett who made the map on p. 149, and to Mr. H. M. McKechnie for all he has done in seeing the book through the press. Lastly, there is a debt to another friend, R. F. I. Bunn : it is not easy to specify, and he is probably quite unaware of its existence, but it is far from small.

Only a minor part of the Stubs records, housed in the Lewis Library of the University of Manchester, has been drawn on for this study. Many account books and many thousands of letters relating to the years 1806–30 await the student who has the enthusiasm and tenacity necessary for research of this kind.

T. S. ASHTON.

February, 1939.

CHAPTER ONE •

INTRODUCTION

As the result of a number of monographs published in the last twenty years the main features of the Industrial Revolution are becoming clear. No systematic study, however, has yet been made of the trades which supplied the new race of artisans and factory workers with the tools without which the machine age could not have come into being. To make such a study would involve years of research in many different areas, and would probably be beyond the powers of any one student. This book must be regarded as merely a small contribution to what must be a co-operative enterprise : its scope is limited to the story of a single business, in one of several centres of the metal-working trades, for a limited period of years.

Peter Stubs was born on 15 June, 1756, the son of John Stubs and the grandson of Ireland Stubs, both of whom followed the calling of currier at Warrington. His father had married, at the age of nineteen, Mary, daughter of Peter Johnson, yeoman of Orford, and had died, less than two years later, in 1757. His grandfather survived till 1763, but Peter was still too young to enter the family business, which probably then came to an end. By what steps he found his vocation we have no means of knowing. All that can be said is that in 1777, when, at the age of twenty-one, he married Mary, daughter of Thomas Sutton of Warrington, he was already established as a file-maker ; that his business was then on a small scale ; that by the age of thirty-one (how much earlier is not known) he had become the landlord of the *White Bear Inn* in Bridge Street, where he still carried on the manufacture of files ; that in 1802 he set up substantial workshops and warehouses, which still stand in what is now known as Scotland Road ; and that he died, at the age of forty-nine, rich not only in substance but also in progeny, for he was the father of eighteen children, and thirteen of these survived him. His business records, almost embarrassing as they are in volume, tell us little about the man himself. But there is evidence that he was shrewd and enterprising, that he shared the robust recreations of his clients at the *White Bear*, that he was a devoted husband and father, and that he was kindly in his treatment of those who worked for him. He was baptized into the Church of England on 4 July, 1756, and he was buried in the parish churchyard at Warrington on 28 February, 1806.

The time and place in which Peter Stubs' life was set were auspicious for a career in industry. In the mid-eighteenth century, workers in iron and steel were scattered about the country almost as widely as workers in the textile trades : nearly every village had its smith. But, as with textiles, there were areas of special concentration : Birmingham, Sheffield, Newcastle-upon-Tyne and, needless to say, London, each had its community of blacksmiths, whitesmiths, cutlers, tool-makers or millwrights, and its merchants supplying their needs or disposing of their products. The metal trades of south-west Lancashire had no single clearly defined centre ; but Warrington might well have appeared to be one in the making. It was on the highroad from London to Carlisle and Scotland, and on the cross-road from Chester to York. It was in close proximity to a coalfield. It was at the head of the tidal waters of a river at the lowest point at which this was crossed by a bridge. The Mersey Navigation gave it access, on the one hand to Liverpool, with its tool-makers, ship-wrights and merchants, and on the other to Manchester, with its rapidly expanding cotton industry ; and a mile and a half to the south was the Bridgewater Canal, by which the town was connected with the whole system of inland navigation. Perhaps it was the very profusion of its activities that prevented its becoming a metal centre comparable to the other towns mentioned ; for besides fabricating tools and casting iron, it made glass and linen and sailcloth, watch-parts, pins and wire, and it was renowned for the quality of its malt and ales.

The metal trades of Warrington and neighbouring places like Prescot (which specialized in watch-parts), Chowbent and Leigh (which made nails) and Ashton-in-Makerfield (which concentrated on locks and hinges) had been long established, and the craftsmen of this region were renowned for their skill. " The tools made in Lancashire are the best executed," wrote a celebrated London watch-maker [1] in 1773, " and if the workmen would please to reason a little, and make them with a little more judgment, we should have no occasion for any foreign production in our shops." Sixty years later a similar tribute was paid to the quality of Lancashire tools. " Under this comprehensive designation ", wrote Dr. Dionysius Lardner,[2] in

[1] Thomas Hutton : *An Introduction to the Mechanical Part of Clock and Watch Work*, 382.

[2] *The Cabinet Cyclopædia : Manufactures in Metal* (1833), Vol. II, Iron and Steel, 318.

1833, " is comprised an immense variety of articles, chiefly used in the manipulatory processes, by almost every class of artificers in this country, and, indeed, by many persons beyond it. The acknowledged superiority of the Lancashire files has been already mentioned, as well as the fact, that such superiority belongs less to the material than to the methods of workmanship. To files may be added chisels, graving, watch and clock makers' tools, hand vices, pincers, metal and wire gauges, cutting pliers, and an extensive variety of articles, of which the foregoing may be taken as specimens. The metropolis of this trade is Warrington, where, in the old-established manufactory of Stubs, every one of the numerous articles sold under the name of ' tools ', in the common meaning of the term, is produced in a style of perfection not, probably, to be surpassed in the world. In this line even Birmingham yields the palm of superiority to Warrington." The high quality of the work of the firm of Stubs is attested also by a practical engineer, James Nasmyth,[1] who remarked that " The ' P.S.' or Peter Stubbs's [sic] files, were so vastly superior to other files, both in the superiority of the steel and in the perfection of the cutting, which long retained its efficiency, that every workman gloried in the possession and use of such durable tools."

The manufacture of these files, as practised during the lifetime of Peter Stubs, involved a long chain of separate processes. Rods of steel, of a cross-section appropriate to the particular size of file to be made, were first cut into suitable lengths and forged into blanks. For this operation the equipment consisted of a hearth, an anvil, a hammer and " swages " or dies, made of tempered steel, and formed like the head of a hammer.[2] One of the swages, grooved to the shape of the back of the file, was fixed to the anvil ; the other, hollowed to the shape of the face of the file, was held in position above this. After heating the piece of rod-steel at his hearth, the forger placed it on the lower swage, and, by striking the back of the upper swage with his hammer, quickly brought the steel to the required form. Next, the scale was removed from the blanks by grinding, and slight

[1] *James Nasmyth, Engineer, An Autobiography* (Pop. edition, 1912), 206.
[2] D. Lardner : *loc. cit.*, 126. Much care and skill were needed in making the swages. In a letter of 13 December, 1793, a Sheffield steel-maker, John Harrison, gave Stubs the benefit of his experience : " Would have you to try the Cast Steel made for Mill Picks for your swages, as can send you a little of what we call Newcastle. . . . We make use of the Mill Pick sort for our swages and harden them only on the face without dipping them in the water wholly and then turn them brown or blue in the temper as suits our purpose."

irregularities were smoothed away by " stripping " the surface with a large " pottance " file. The blanks were then annealed by bringing them to a red heat and allowing them to cool slowly so that they would offer a surface soft enough to take the chisel. After this came the all-important operation of cutting. The blank was held in position by leather stirrups on a bed of pewter, the purpose of which was to reduce the recoil from the blow of the hammer on the chisel and to preserve the cut face of the file from injury when the reverse side was being cut. The file-cutter sat by the bench, or stood, his left foot on a block of stone, and his left elbow resting on the bent knee, so as to steady the hand that held the chisel and keep the vertical inclination of the tool unchanged. With the hammer held in his right hand he gave the chisel a blow, then raised the chisel, drew it back a minute distance, and slid it forward until he could feel the tiny ridge made by the last cut, before giving the next blow. But so rapidly did these movements follow one another that it was impossible for the eye to distinguish them : the speed with which the series of uniform cuts appeared on the surface of the blank was the result of a high degree of muscular co-ordination, and such skill came only of a long apprenticeship to the craft. Files may be single-cut or cross-cut : that is to say, they may have only one course of parallel indentations across the surface or they may have two courses intersecting each other. In making a cross-cut file, when the first course of teeth had been cut it was, necessary to strip away irregularities with a pottance file, so that the chisel might glide easily over the surface at the second cutting. After completing this, the cutter stamped the initials *P.S.* on the heel, or tang, and the file was then passed on to the workers in the hardening-room.

Here the file was first rubbed with charcoal to remove any particles of steel or pewter from the teeth, and covered with paste in order to preserve it from damage. At this point the reason why Peter Stubs combined two such apparently disparate occupations as file-making and inn-keeping becomes clear.[1] For the paste he used consisted of malt dust and " barm-bottoms ", the dregs of beer barrels ; and it has been suggested that carbon from these ingredients was made to enter the teeth of the file, so giving them greater durability and strength.[2] Hardening consisted of bringing the file to red heat and

[1] Such a combination of trades was not unique. *Gore's Liverpool Directory* for 1769, 1773 and 1774 included the name of William Gibson " victualler and file cutter " and that for 1773 the name of Thomas Tarbuck, " file cutter and victualler ".

[2] Barm-bottoms were used for this purpose till late in the nineteenth century, as is proved by entries in the books of the concern.

then thrusting it into a solution of salt and water. This operation, like that of cutting, was a delicate one : files of some shapes had to be immersed quickly, those of other shapes slowly ; some had to be held vertically in the solution, others obliquely. It was important, moreover, that, at the instant of dipping, the files should be at just the correct temperature : unless judgment were exercised here the result might be a faulty or misshapen product ; and customers were rightly concerned that special care should be taken at this stage. " Will thank you to give the old hardener 1s. to drink and charge it to our act:", wrote J. Weston of Coventry, in October, 1796, " Desire him to temper them well as we have had some complaints of them being too soft." After hardening, all that remained was to test the files, oil them to prevent rust, wrap them in stout paper, and pack them in wooden boxes. A London ironmonger, Thomas Jackson, complained, in May, 1795, that the files sent him had been spoilt because they had not been oiled ; and in November, 1797, Harwood & Thomas of Sheffield sent back a parcel of files which had gone rusty owing to their having been packed in paper of inferior quality.

This is not a technical treatise and no attempt will be made to describe the processes of work in further detail. Nor is it necessary to say much of the varieties of product. Suffice it to mention that files may be of many different lengths, sections and cuts. The various types owe their names either to the use to which they are to be put (as, for example, watch-files, dentists' files, pit-saw and frame-saw files) ; to the shape (taper, blunt or equalling, i.e. of the same thickness from point to heel) ; to the transverse section (flat, round, triangular, square) ; or to the cut (rough, bastard, smooth, super). At one time or other Stubs made, or supplied, files of almost every kind ; but, throughout, his speciality was the relatively small, high-grade file required by clock-makers, whitesmiths, machine-makers and cotton-spinners. When customers asked for larger files he obtained them from other makers and generally from his friends in Sheffield.[1]

In the early years of his enterprise Stubs almost certainly made the files from start to finish. The earliest records are in four small books, each consisting of fewer than twenty pages, containing loosely kept

---

[1] This incomplete account of the operations of file-making and of the types of files is drawn partly from evidence in the documents themselves, partly from printed works—notably G. H. Lloyd : *The Cutlery Trades* and *A Treatise on Files and Rasps*, published by the Nicholson File Co., Rhode Island, U.S.A. (1878). Information has also been supplied by Mr. F. Aylmer Frost, a descendant of Peter Stubs and a director of the business, as well as by Mr. Robert Ward of Sheffield, a friend and former pupil of the author, who began his working life as a file-cutter.

accounts of work done and payments received. They exhibit Peter Stubs as a small master, making files to the order of merchants or manufacturers who usually supplied him with steel and, occasionally, with tools. The workshop must have been small, for only one apprentice was employed, though a man named Benjamin—probably Benjamin Jolley—assisted now and then and was paid at the rate of 1s. 8d. a day. The first entry is dated 11 December, 1776 ; but, since it records a balance of 10d. due to him, it is clear that Stubs must have set up in the trade before that date. During the following year he worked mainly to the order of a William Barrow of Prescot, for whom between 23 January and 27 December he made 209 dozen files of various types, delivering them either by the hand of his apprentice or through the post. Stubs appears to have provided the steel and to have allowed Barrow to keep a running account. Barrow was debited with the finished work and credited with round sums which, from time to time, he remitted in cash or bills ; at the end of two or three months the account was made up and any balance outstanding was either settled or carried forward to the next account. With other customers, however, the practice was somewhat different. Chorley & Leech, wholesale ironmongers of Ashton-in-Makerfield, usually sent supplies of steel, together with pottance files for stripping, with each order, and deducted the value of these when they made payment on delivery of the files. In all cases the files were sold by Stubs at current retail prices, less a discount which seems to have varied with the customer and the size of the order : Barrow was allowed 25 per cent., Chorley & Leech 20 per cent., and others, whose orders were small, 10 per cent.

From 1776 to 1782 there was little change of circumstance. Gradually the circle of customers widened. In 1777 orders were received from Chorley & Watson and Wyke & Green,[1] in 1778 from Thomas Houghton[2] ; in 1779 from Samuel Parry and Joseph Flitcroft ; and in 1780 from Mr. Peck, Mr. Kendrick and a James Crookes, who, on one occasion, instructed Stubs to send the files to Joseph Roberts of Birmingham. In 1781, Chorley & Harrison and Chorley & Leech

---

[1] In *Gore's Liverpool Directory* for 1774 Wyke & Green are described as " watch makers &c.", and their address is given as Wyke's Court, Dale Street, Liverpool. In Wyke's Court there worked also J. Appleton, watch-tool maker, John Kaye, clockmaker, and John Wyke, watchmaker. The firm of Wyke & Green was begun by John Wyke of Prescot, who issued a tool catalogue about 1760. See *Hist. Soc. Lancs. and Cheshire*, vi. 66.

[2] Perhaps of Liverpool. The name Thomas Houghton, ironmonger, of Preeson's Row appears in *Gore's Liverpool Directory* for 1773.

sent long orders, divided into sections, each of which related to a particular customer of their own ; and new names, such as those of a Mr. Collier, and Thomas Tarbuck,[1] appear in the accounts. A Mr. Wairing [2] bought files in small quantities for himself as well as for Peter Litherland—almost certainly the Litherland who acquired fame for the improvements he made in the lever watch.

Generally payment was made in cash. But occasional debit items appear against Stubs not only for steel, tools and oilstones, but also for clothing. In November, 1779, for example, William Barrow supplied two fents of velveret, valued at 6s. 7d. ; and in May, 1781, Wyke & Green of Liverpool, who (as will be seen later) were given to such practices, paid a debt of £4 7s. 10d. by supplying materials for a new suit.[3] There is no indication, however, that Stubs was subjected to the evil of truck on any significant scale ; for his work was not confined to the orders of any single factor and this no doubt placed him in a position of relative independence. He was able to lend small sums to a Mr. Howard who supplied him with steel [4] ; in 1779 he advanced £2 1s. to Samuel Griffiths on the security of goods ; and that he was something more than a mere outworker is also suggested by his accepting payment from Barrow in the form of bills. Almost the last entry in these books shows that he was, indeed, in a position to give credit to his customers : it relates to an order for files worth £5 18s. 6d. which a Peter Atherton had instructed him to send by coach to London. Stubs drew a bill on Atherton at one month, dated 2 April, 1782.

Nevertheless, his resources cannot have been large. Perhaps it was poverty as well as piety that led him, in June, 1778, to bring his grandmother, Mrs. Johnson, to his house ; for she paid for her board.

[1] Thomas Tarbuck was the file-cutter and victualler of Liverpool referred to *supra*, 4 n.

[2] Perhaps Thomas Wareing, merchant, of 35 Lord Street, Liverpool. —*Gore's Liverpool Directory*, 1774.

[3] The statement includes a " Turkey oile stone " priced at 4s. 3d. The other items are as follows : 1 hat 11s. 6d. ; $2\frac{6}{16}$ yds. of fine broadcloth at 18s. a yard ; 4½ yds. of Shalloon at 19d. a yard ; 14 coat buttons at 1½d. each ; 1 doz. breast buttons at 9d. the dozen ; 2 pairs of brown thread hose at 2s. 10d. each. The balance was made up of Calimanca and hose valued at 19s. 2½d.

[4] Mr. Howard is credited with the sums due to Benjamin for the occasional help he gave Stubs. It thus appears that Benjamin was an employee of Howard. On one occasion in 1777 Howard was credited " By Benjamin 2 hrs. & half 4d." Since, when he worked for a full day, Howard was credited with 1s. 8d., it would seem that the day's work was of 12½ hours.

B

Some months later he provided lodgings for his brother-in-law, Samuel Sutton, who repaid the debt so incurred by soling shoes for Stubs and his wife. And a clear indication that the family means were far from ample is given by a bill, covering eighteen weeks, for sums owing to Mrs. Stubs for washing clothes (shirts at 2*d*. each, stocks at ½*d*.). Altogether the amount due came to 12*s*. 11½*d*. : it was payable by a Mary Sutton, and, since this was also her own maiden name, it seems likely that Mrs. Stubs was doing the washing for her mother. An entry of 29 January, 1781, " Then Edward Nangreaves came to our house to Nurse " suggests yet another way in which Mary Stubs may have supplemented her husband's earnings in these early years.

The record is fragmentary. But it gives some indication of the process by which a young man of energy might advance from humble beginnings in the Lancashire tool trade. Clear and careful handwriting was at that time a factor of importance in commercial success ; and evidence of the struggle for self-improvement in this direction is to be found in odd corners of the account books, where such phrases as " My Kingdom for an Horse said King Richard " are inscribed in penmanship of almost painful accuracy. Having learnt how to make files of high quality, Stubs was preparing himself for the equally important task of building up a business connection for their sale.

CHAPTER TWO

THE WORKERS

I

WHEN Peter Stubs next comes to view in 1788 he is the tenant of the *White Bear Inn*, in Bridge Street, Warrington. Here he combines the activity of innkeeper, maltster, and brewer with that of file-maker on a much larger scale than six years earlier. Bills for the repair of the property suggest that he had workshops and a smithy near at hand—possibly in the inn-yard itself. And a Workmen's Book, the first entries in which are dated January, 1788, shows that he was employing file-workers, not only in Warrington, but also in other places in the south-west of Lancashire and the neighbouring parts of Cheshire. Relations with these workers were very similar to those which had formerly existed between the factors and Stubs himself. Steel, pewter, malt dust, oil and pottance files were supplied to the outworkers ; and each week or fortnight the finished files were brought in and the file-makers were credited with their value, less a discount of 25 per cent. Payments to cover the immediate needs of the workers were made weekly, fortnightly, or sometimes at irregular intervals ; but a final settlement generally took place only after the lapse of some months. At such settlement the costs of the materials and tools advanced, together with the interim payments, were deducted from the value of the work done and the balance was paid in cash. And if, as frequently happened, the balance were adverse to the worker, the amount owed to Stubs was carried forward to a new account.

A few examples will suffice. On 20 January, 1788, Thomas and William Appleton of Huyton were given 1 cwt. 1 qr. 4 lb. of cast steel, which (at 7½d. per lb.) was valued at £4 10s., together with two files, charged at 1s. 0½d. At the end of the week they brought back 18 dozen hand-saw and frame-saw files reckoned, after deduction of discount, at £1 16s. They received, however, in cash only £1 5s. In the following week they were supplied with 2 qrs. 2¾ lb. of steel and two more files ; and when, at the end of the week, they returned finished goods of a net value of £4 7s. 11d. they received £3 5s. 11d. The same procedure was followed each week until 16 March when

9

the account was settled by the payment of a balance of £2 1s. 5½d. due to the Appletons.

In this instance the account was balanced after eight weeks ; the next, which was opened immediately on 17 March, was settled four weeks later ; but sometimes more than twelve months elapsed before a reckoning was made. In the first period of eight weeks the net amount received by the Appletons was £18 5s. 3d., and in a period of twenty-five weeks beginning 28 September, 1788, their cash receipts were £63 11s. 4d., in addition to small payments in malt and hops. It would not be safe, however, to draw from such figures any inference as to total net earnings ; for we know nothing, on the one hand, of the outgoings for fuel and rent of the workshop, or, on the other hand, of any orders the Appletons may have had from other employers. The working group seems to have consisted of four members, for on 21 March, 1789, separate accounts were opened for James Appleton, Thomas Appleton, William Appleton, junior, and William Appleton, senior. That one at least of these men was dependent on Stubs for capital is proved by entries debiting James with an anvil at £1, a new pair of bellows at 3 guineas, and a Turkey oilstone at 10s. ; and a separate (undated) document debits a Martha Appleton with an anvil at 2 guineas, a swaging anvil at 15s., a vice at 10s., two file-cutter's benches at 4s. each, and 45 lb. of steel at 7½d. per lb.

The Workmen's Book, which covers the years 1788–92, contains the accounts of six or seven other outworkers who made files for Stubs. One of these, William Taylor, was already in debt to the extent of £3 13s. when his account opened on 3 April, 1788, and at no time during the four years did he succeed in turning his debit into a credit balance. Every ten or fourteen days cash was paid to him or to his wife (who perhaps carried the files to the *White Bear*) and from time to time Taylor was debited with a cask of beer or a cheese, supplied by Stubs.[1] When James Plumpton of Ditton began work on 11 May, 1789, he borrowed £5 immediately and 12s. four days later ; and, like Taylor, at no time before the last account closed was he out of debt to his employer. For three other file-makers, John Prescott and William Molyneux of Rainhill and Peter Whitfield of Ditton, the accounts are short : letters from them make

			£	s.	d.
[1]	7 Feb. 1789	To 1 Barrel Beer	0	2	3
	12 Mar. 1789	To 9 galls. Beer at 3d.	0	2	3
	12 Nov. 1790	To 1 Cheese weight			
		34¼ lb. at 4¼d.	0	12	1½

it clear that their work for Stubs was casual and that they had normally other sources of employment.[1] It seems probable that all these men made files from start to finish ; but another Molyneux, whose Christian name was James and who lived at Prescot, apparently specialized in the process of cutting, for from November, 1791, Stubs began to send him blanks, instead of steel in the form of rods. In 1792 a son of this Molyneux arranged to work for Stubs in Warrington ; but a number of letters show that he had obtained employment at weekly wages with John and Thomas Johnson of Prescot, who refused to release him. The fact that the lad had broken his arm (and a letter from his father saying " if he coms to work with you I am afraid he will do you littl servis for I believe there is no truth in him ") may have consoled Stubs for the broken engagement.

It is, however, the relations with yet another outworker, Carolus Charles of Aughton, that are most informative of conditions of labour in the industry at this period. The connection seems to have begun on 27 March, 1789, when, as the Workmen's Book shows, Charles was given 27 lb. of cast steel to work into frame-saw files. During the following years he executed other occasional orders ; but his letters show that he was tied by debt to another firm of tool-makers, Wyke & Green of Liverpool, to whom reference was made in the previous chapter. Charles was anxious to work for Stubs ; he was willing to transfer to him his rights to the labour of his sons, who were apprenticed to their father ; and, as an inducement, he offered to supply Stubs with fourteen unhardened, or thirteen hardened files, for the price usually paid for twelve.[2]

AUGHTON *Octr. 1st 1791.*

SR.,

I wrote to you some time since but no answer, the subject of which was as follows viz. to desire to know if you can give me work if it be for 2 or 3 months only, or till May next at which time if it be agreeable I propose comeing to Warrington to reside and harden or finish for you if you want one at that time and if you think proper will turn my lads over or if you can give [me] sufficient work in your Shop will keep 'em on their time out, at the rates you give others, they are forwards in their business and works very well. If you can give me work here till May (as I can't leave here before) you may be assured I shall come to War-

---

[1] William Molyneux was a master-manufacturer whose reputation for quality stood as high as that of Peter Stubs.

[2] The practice of giving more than twelve to a dozen was strongly condemned by the workers in Sheffield. It was denounced by the versifier, Joseph Mather, in his *Watkinson and his Thirteens* :
    " May those be transported or sent for marines
    That works for big W——n at his thirteens."

rington. I shall send 'em if I send any soft 14 to doz., and propose finishing by the doz. which I think is more satisfaction to both sides. I paid the person for the last [? letter] being a private but I suppose it was not deliver'd and will pay for this. Beg you'll keep this a profound secret as I've been told in Greens warehouse of alowing you 13 to doz. hard but thought others did the same, and particularly desire you'll send by return of Post as I shall be in Liverpool on Wednesday next and you'll oblige you Hble Servt.

CAROLUS CHARLES.

P.S. Direct for me to be left with Jn. Collins, Brewer at beesam and Shuffle in Cheapside Liverpool.

Evidently Stubs acceded to the request for employment, for the Workmen's Book shows that on 7 November he directed $46\frac{1}{4}$ lb. of cast steel to Charles. The following letters and extracts need little comment. They throw light on the plight of a domestic worker bound by debt to a hard employer, and they afford evidence of the pernicious effects of payment by truck.

AUGHTON 1st Jan. '92.

SR.,

I hope you'll Excuse this as I did Expect your writing the week after I was with you, but hope there is Nothing amiss. Mr. Green has not been at home some time before I was with you nor is he yet come or I wou'd not have troubled you and beg you'll be kind enough to send me an order and Steel, and if you'll oblige me with 4 or 5 guineas shall forever remember it and send your work in small parcels or by any stated time you choose. I have money to pay to Different people and Can't get it from 'em. Yesterday week I had not my due by near half, yesterday the same. He will pay only 10s. pound of the Clear neat Cash when all is Deducted, and I can't take truck for the remaider at his price. H. Yond told my wife yesterday that one of the men in your Shop told him you and I had been makeing an agreement and I was to go to Warrington to work Constantly for you, by which you may se how Dagerous 'tis to trust Some people, not that I value it if Green know it, but wou'd advise you to take care who you Confide in, but beg and Desire you'll asaist me in the above friendship and I will give Joseph Henshaw meeting on purpose at Liverpool on Thursday next. Pray don't Sr. don't Disapoint your friend.

Cs. CHARLES.

I've paid Carriage.

Joseph Henshaw (or Henshall) was the carrier. Charles was anxious that his employer should remain ignorant of his dealings with Stubs ; and a week later, on 8 January, he expressed his fears lest information should reach Green by Henshall or some other person : " There is apparently a Combination against me by some of Molyneux's family, the Carrier and Mr. Green. Henshaw has a lad bound to Jno.

Prescot whose wife has an Inveterate Hatred against me but don't know for what. Therefore Caution is doubly to be observ'd, lest Henshaw let them know, and they Mr. Green know, of any Concerns 'twixt us." He begged Stubs to send him an order and some cash, adding " Mr. Green's not being at home throws me. I cou'd [get] but little cash and no goods except wholly instead of cash."

AUGHTON 18 Jan. '92.

SIR,

I received the Steel on Saturday last. I have had not any by me Strong Enough for any but the 5 In. Cross which was in hand before I received it, but my son being taken bad of the bloody flux will throw us a little behind but you may Depend we shall do 'em without Omision now he is gotten better. I can't tell how long they will be in executeing being larger than I ever made any in Lancashire. I am sorry you took Umbrage at my Desireing 4 or 5 guineas. I did not expect it from the acquaintance we have had but when a man is Driven to necessity and near to Desperation I hope you'll excuse the attempt. I think I shall send them by another Hand than Henshaw. I was right in my Conjectures about the Combination but no more of that now. I've a Settlement with Mr. Green and if I must leave him wou'd Desire to do it honourably and quietly as we met so. Will let you know a day or two before the files comes. I cou'd be of great utility to you if things wou'd suit but more of that another time. I don't know the price of the large Cross but shall rely on you for that.

I am
Sr. your Hble Servt.
CS. CHARLES.

P.S. I am more free from Mr. Green by either tye or promise than I am from you, but shou'd not like any transactions betwixt you and I ever turn'd over. I want to get a Settlement without passion.

AUGHTON July 7th '92.

SR.,

I've sent you the following files viz,

12 doz. frame Saw 5 In. @ 4/- p	2 – 8 – 0			
13 doz. Do. Do. 4½ In. @ 3/6 p	2 – 5 – 6			
2 doz. Do. Do. 4 In. @ 3/- p	0 – 6 – 0	7 – 8 – 6		
12 doz. Hand Do. 4½ In. 3/6 p	2 – 2 – 0	1 – 17 – 1½		
6 Cross files 6 In. bast. 6/- p	0 – 3 – 0			
6 Do. Do. 7 In. Do. 8/- p	0 – 4 – 0	5 – 11 – 4½		

7 – 8 – 6

There is 14 Cross in both sizes. I have more but tyd them in dry'd paper and they've Contracted rust & are spoil'd, these was put in Oily paper and are saved. If you please shou'd be glad you'd send 4 guineas by Sherwood on Tuesday made in a parcel, and the box. I shou'd have sent more files but my son was so put out of the way by his bror. Joseph by being struck and shaked in such a manner by him when I was Absent that I thought for 3 days had not ever seen thro' it, he not being in a Capacity to bear it. Joseph went from here on Saturday last to bring work to Prescot but has not been seen here since. As he has threaten'd little Cranage I suppose he has been with you, which if he has shou'd be glad you'd let me know and how they've order'd as his Mother says he shall not go to him any more and is quite Inconsoliable, have not much time now but think I shall remove from here sooner than thought of. This you'll keep, but think to come over again to Warrington to'ards Michealmas and by then shall be more settled in some points. Am Sr. with Due respect (not forgetting your favours)

> Subscribe myself your Hble Servt.   Cs. CHARLES.
> I think there is 2 or 3 of 5 In. frame Saw among 4½.

AUGHTON *July 21st.* '92.

SR.,

I am sorry there was any mistake in the 4 In. frame saw files. Was you not mistaken in booking 'em, as I know there was no more than you mention'd, have sent you the following files [*Here follows a bill for 52 doz. files valued at £11 9s. od., less discount £2 17s. od.*] Desire if you please to remit me 6 guineas. Let me know if you be willing for Sherwood to Carry the files. Hie proposes Carrying them at 6d. a time. Have had another summons from Mr. Green. I believe he is very Ill at want for files and wonders I neglected him so long. If he searches his breast he may soon know, says he will either come or send if I don't send him an Explanation in a little time and heard he is for bringing an Exorbitant bill against me. His way of tradeing has been very Intricate. When any cash of any Acct. was to [be] paid he neither cou'd nor wou'd he said pay it Stormingly saying I pay you more money than any one, then paying what he thought proper which caused people to take his goods which price 'tis two to one you cou'd not get and if Importuned for a bill fly in a passion and tell you he had more plague with [you] than any body else after you had travel'd ten or 12 Miles in the night and not a dry thread on you & set in his Warehouse for 6 or 7 hours without being ask'd what you want. I wish I was well out of his Clutches or power for I suppose I must have little Content till I am. Shou'd be glad of your Advice on Tuesday as I think to give him some Sort of an answer and shou'd be glad you'd put the paper into the box & make the Cash into a parcel and you'll oblige Sr. yr. Hble Servt

> Cs. CHARLES.

Evidently Green was taking full advantage of his position as creditor. In a letter to Stubs of 4 August, 1792, Charles says he had offered to pay in instalments of half a guinea one week and a guinea another or three guineas a month, but that Green insisted on payment of the whole debt immediately :

. . . the sum, Sr., is too large for me to have the presumption to think any one will advance it for me. I know he wants the work worse than Cash by which he thinks to put you or some one else to a nonplus. He is not sure I work all for you. I beg you'll let me know if I may expect to be reinstated with you when I've Clear'd him which shall be as quick as possible, and will work for you as often as I can in the mean time. I will work this steel up before I do ought for him . . .

From this point a personal tragedy takes precedence of the financial problem. A letter from Charles, dated 17 August, 1792, contains the following passage :

I think as this last Steel is not open'd if you send me 5 guineas the remaining part will about settle for last steel and pay £1-0-0 for Stopage to agreement &c. You see the difference of quantity thro' my being from home, they've done very little that while and have been taken off since thro' this graceless son of mine and am afraid I shall be taken off again thro' his abuseing my landlord near 60 years of age by strikeing him in a Cruel manner by which he has broke 2 of his ribs. The docter thinks he can't mend. Whether he is gone off or no I can't tell, but his wife and son vows revenge against him whether he dies or lives. He thought to have lived here without paying any rent and to perplex me. . . .

In the New Year there was worse news of the son's behaviour : in the course of a letter dated 22 January, 1793, Charles apologizes for being behind with his work and says :

I realy was very bad a fortnight since in so much that I was past speaking, but thanks to God 'tis gone off only has left a deep and heavy sighing which gives me ease. . . . My son Joseph writes me word this Day. He has live'd above 2 weeks Chiefly on bread and water, only one penny worth of butter p. Day which is oweing to miscarriage of Cash that has been sent by different Contributions. His prosecutor is Daughter of Richd. Norkert Coach maker with Mr. Cooper in Manchester and gone home and how to know Whether they will appear against him or no can't tell but suppose both him and others will Expect me to go to the Assizes which will be an Expensive affair. Should be glad of your advice likewise Secrecy.

On 5 February further details of the miserable affair are disclosed :

My son is Confin'd by a woman who has sworn a rape against him but don't think he is guilty of any such thing. He writes a most lamentable letter and is greatly afraid of his life and yet writes in a stupid stiff manner scorning to bend or behave as he ought, never once mentioning his duty or Love to Father, Mother, Sister or bror. now writes for 3 guineas to fee Council and wants me to go. If he can't have it he fears his life is gone if the wench appears, and threatens Distantly his own life . . . how for to act I don't know, he has been a bad son to me and wrong'd me of a deal, and 3 guineas with loss of time &c. will be heavier than I can bear . . .

A fortnight later Charles told Stubs that Cooper's business had failed (presumably in the crisis that accompanied the outbreak of war) and that he had been told Norkert had " gone to London for life as he dar not come to Liverpool ". He begs Stubs to " enquire minutely and very cunningly " if this is so. On 1 March he asks for the loan of four guineas and for the payment of four and a half guineas due for work done, promising to repay the loan by instalments " by the 40 weeks are up "—a phrase which implies that he had bound himself to Stubs for this period. His persecution mania is again revealed in his request that the $4\frac{1}{2}$ guineas should be sent openly by the hand of Sherwood, the carrier, but that the 4 guineas constituting the loan should " be made up in straw in the box for Secrecy ". He announces that he must go to the Assizes " or people seems to cry a shame ", but adds that he will travel before daybreak. On 23 March he writes, " I've not work'd but 2 days these 3 weeks nor I realy think the poor boys cou'd not work so great has been my sorrow that I am nearly destroy'd." And on 6 April he informs Stubs that his son Joseph still protests his innocence though the death warrant has been signed. " He says he is reconciled to his fate and begs pardon of us all for the wrong done us by him . . . he begs if anyone upbraid us with it for heaven's sake not to shew any resentment and says the Lord will do that for me so that it gives me a little ease as I think he is firmly attached to and puts all Confidence above. I've spare'd neither pains nor Expense so my heart is Clear and Conscience also." A few days later Joseph Charles was hanged.[1]

Carolus Charles probably belonged to a social stratum a little above that of the other outworkers—as, indeed, the phrasing of his letters suggests.[2] A letter of September, 1792, mentions that he employed three lads, and another of the following month informs Stubs that he was thinking of hiring a fourth. It seems likely that he had once been a master manufacturer making files for customers on his own account, for on 13 November, 1792, he writes to say that, since he is now engaged to Stubs, he is passing on an order he has received from one William Sparrow, an ironmonger of Wolverhampton, with whom

[1] " On Thursday se'nnight Joseph Charles was executed at Lancaster pursuant to his sentence, for a rape."—*Manchester Mercury*, 16 April, 1793.

[2] He was perhaps a relative of Joseph Charles, file-cutter, of Vernon Street, Liverpool, whose name appears in the Liverpool Directories of 1769, 1773, and 1774.

Stubs subsequently did a considerable trade. His story serves as a reminder that the fluidity of factors of production which was so marked a feature of the metal trades at this time could operate to depress, as well as to raise, the economic status of the craftsman.

II

Unfortunately the Workmen's Books for the next few years are missing. But occasional letters from other outworkers throw further light on the dependence of the domestic file-maker upon his employer. The three that follow are from a man who, like Carolus Charles, was anxious to free himself from Green of Liverpool : his resources were obviously small, for Stubs had to supply him with tools and pewter as well as with steel.[1]

June the 11 1794.

Sr.,
    I take opportunet to rite to you and wdd. be obliged to you if you wdd. send me a little work and hope you will not take it amiss at my sending to you for I shud be glad to sarve you unnone to Mister Green at present. If you will due me the fever prey send me a anser. Derect your Letter to

Thomas Tatlock
number 10 plum Street
Liverpool.

Liverpool *September 20th,* 1795.

Dear Sir,
    I have made **bold** to write a few lines to you to beg the favour for you to have lent me three or four guineas. At this present time we are rather in distress or els would not have troubled you. It is to pay a few trifling debts with. You may depend upon me paying you every peny again by stoping so much a week. I am now working the last of your work up. I hope you be so good as to send me more work and to have granted me this one favor and you will greatly oblige me. You may stop it as you please. I received your letter and the money with great satisfaction and I hope while I have my health to do my best for you in every point. So no more at present from your obedient servant

Thomas Tatlock.

Liverpool, *April ye 9th* 1796.

Sir,
    I take the liberty to in form you that this day my wife is got to her bed some time before we expected and as my rent is due it has put me to a great streat as my landlord cannot do without it. I shall take it as a great favour if you will assist me with 2 pound ten shillings and

---

[1] As shown by a letter of 6 December, 1795.

if you will please to send me word how much you will chuse me to pay a week I will pay it with pleasure. I am sorry that you found fault with the work but I altered my swage to your patern and no one cuts them but my self and the young man but I will do my endeavour to plese you and I hope that you will plese to send me the sum mentioned which I shall acknolage as a great favour from

Your Humble Servant
THOMAS TATLOCK.

The same domestic incident was the occasion of a request for money from another Liverpool worker :

LIVERPOOL   March 16, 1795.

SIR,
£ s.
I desire you will oblige me with a little cash to the amount of 1 10 as I am at present in want of some and my work is not quit finished and you may send it by Mr. Sherwood which you will greatly oblige your humble Sert.

WILLIAM LANCELOT.

Sir this is to inform you that my wife is deliver'd of a child and I shall be glad if you will assist me at this time.

Other outworkers who made files for Stubs in the 'nineties were Jonathan Cranage of Aughton, Richard Hayes of Widnes and John Chadbond of Ashton-in-Makerfield. The last of these was clearly an independent producer with connections of his own ; for when, on 17 May, 1795, he sent a sample dozen of 12-inch files and invited orders for more, he asked Stubs to supply him with a dozen smaller files which he had to deliver to a cotton factory. During the following five years he continued to send quantities of large files (usually 12 or 14 inches long) and made occasional purchases of relatively small ones (6–8 inches). Now and then Stubs provided him with small amounts of steel, but generally Chadbond supplied his own. In 1799, when there was a dearth of steel[1] he asked Stubs to return old files for re-cutting—" Look your 12 inch over as will do to cut as there is no steel to be got for to make new ones of at present "— and two months later he wrote, " If you will let me have all the 12 Inch my mark when wore down will give you $3\frac{1}{2}$d. p. lb." It seems likely that he supplied a large part of the pottance files used by Stubs and his workers for stripping. His price for new 12-inch files was 8s., and for re-cut files 4s. a dozen.

If the relations with Chadbond serve to illustrate the tendency to specialization by product, those with others offer examples of specialization by process. A few outworkers, like Carolus Charles, made their files from start to finish ; but usually, it would appear,

---

[1] *Vide infra*, 45.

the cut files were sent back to Stubs to be hardened by an expert in Warrington. Moreover, some workers confined themselves to forging and others to cutting : in April, 1801, a John Heyes of St. Helens sent his apprentice to Stubs with a note asking for forged blanks to cut, adding that he had not had " half imploy this three months " and would soon be in distress, unless Stubs could help him.

In addition to that in files Stubs was doing a considerable business in other Lancashire tools. Some of these he bought from the factors at Ashton and elsewhere, but many of them were made for him by workmen whose conditions of employment were similar to those of the file-makers. In 1792 a John Shaw began to make hammers and pliers to his order, and T. Thompson of Eccleston supplied saws and saw-blades. In June of that year William Arstal of Blackbrook wrote, " I am inform'd you are become buyer of Hand-vices and is at want of good many. I have too Hands at Vice-making . . . If you and I can gree on terms you may have some " ; and in December, 1793, a William Knowles, who was just out of his apprenticeship, offered to supply compasses, callipers and dividers. Next to files, however, it was implements for the use of shoemakers that provided the largest trade. The following letters are from an awl-maker of Stockport, who, it would seem, worked also for Samuel Oldknow, the well-known cotton-spinner and weaver of fine muslins.

SR., I have sent these five Groce. They [are] all the Heel Blads I could get Readey But will send you more on Tuesday by Nields Cart. I sent you 18 Dozen Heal Blads and 12 Dozen sewing a week before. I sent them 6 Groce. If not Recd. them pleas to enquire at Mr. Bowman's. By those Mis carreing you might think I was serveing sumbody else. I do a sure you I do not Receive 1 shilling in all the Town neither will I, so Long as you will imploy mee. I will serve you in the Best manner I can so I hope this will Suffice you at present.

I am yours at Command
JAMES LYON.

October 1795.

STOCKPORT *Decr.* 17, 1795.

MR. STUBS,

Sir, I Rec'd your Letter yesterday. I am in Good Health but have been mutch uneasey at your silence so Long. I thought I had offended that you wou'd not Imploy mee any Longer. I have tould Mr. Ouldknow and hee will give mee work after Christmas. So I intended to a maid you sum work in the Holodays for what I owe you and to a Return'd your Tools. But I will never Leave you while you will Imploy mee. I will never Bastard my Promes to you. Your abstance has been no profit to mee though I have sould sum and I have a Quantaty under hand of most usefull sorts and will Bring you all I

can next week's end.   I must beg you will send mee Letter to Receive
3 Guineas for its a Long time since I Rec'd mutch.   If you will grant
my Desire I will bee under a heavy Stopidge that shall suffice you.   I
will not send any more by any Body for I will Bring them every other
Saterday if God Permit.

> I remain your Hble Srvt.
>
> JAS. LYON.

As will be seen in the following chapter, there was a tendency, as
time went on, for Stubs to bring the scattered file-makers to his own
headquarters in Warrington, where supervision of their work could
be more effectively exercised.   Nevertheless, even in his later years,
he continued to obtain a considerable part of his tools and files from
outsiders—as, indeed, was the practice of his sons and grandsons, long
after his death.   Prominent among the outworkers was the family
of Appletons who, it has been seen, began their association with
Stubs at least as early as 1788.   The Workmen's Day Book, 1802–4,
contains entries relating to no fewer than six Appletons—James,
John (senior), Mary, John (described as " Mary's son "), George and
Peter.   Each of these had separate accounts, though George's was
opened only when that of John (senior) ceased :   probably George
took over the enterprise on the death or retirement of his father.
Considerable differences in the scale of output are revealed by the
accounts.   Normally James delivered each week files valued (after
discount) at between £4 and £5 :   Mary's weekly product was of about
the same size and on one occasion, indeed, it reached a value of over
£8.   Probably both these were themselves employers of labour on a
small scale.   John Appleton (senior), on the other hand, produced
files each week worth only £1 to £1 5s., and the output of Peter and
" John, Mary's son " was normally priced at something less than
£1 :   they probably worked without assistants.   Inspection of the
book discloses some degree of specialization.   Mary's work seems to
have been confined to making frame-saw files of 4–4½ inches, and the
same was true of John (senior) and Peter ;   James and " John, Mary's
son " made also pit saw files of 6 inches and " ruff " and " bastard "
rounding-off files up to 8 inches in length.   All of them were supplied
with steel and tools by Stubs, as well as with wrapping paper.

In addition to the Appletons, some twenty other outworkers were
employed in these years in making files.   Not all of these, however,
were at work at the same time, and although some of them, like
William Dennett of Widnes, undertook to work exclusively for Stubs,[1]
others received only occasional orders.   It would seem probable,

---

[1] He signed an agreement to this effect on 3 May, 1804.

therefore, that the bulk of the output of files now came from Stubs' own shops in Warrington.[1]

Tools of other kinds—pliers, nippers, vices, compasses, dividers, callipers, hammers and saw blades—were, however, still made entirely by outworkers ; and the same was true of the wire, pinions and parts of watches and clocks that were coming to bulk large in the business of the concern. In 1802 or 1803 Stubs began to obtain supplies of wire from William Houghton of Hale Bank, a descendant of the inventor of pinion wire, and thus was established an association between the two businesses that was to endure for more than a century. Another concern with which extensive dealings in tools were carried on was that of John & Thomas Johnson of Fall Lane, Prescot. Their connection with Stubs arose out of an order for 3 dozen eight-day-clock pinions which Stubs had given to a William Miller in 1799 : on 9 May Thomas Johnson wrote to say he had sent the pinions at the request of Miller " as he works almost constantly for me and could not get your Ordr. in your time ". Thereafter the Johnsons supplied a wide variety of clock-makers' tools and clock and watch parts. When they, or one of their sons, brought in the goods Stubs would pay them a round sum of, say, £10, and the balance was allowed to stand over to be settled later. Normally tool-makers supplied their wares at a trade discount of 25 per cent., but the Johnsons allowed only $7\frac{1}{2}$ per cent. off the standard prices ; and when, in June, 1804, Stubs attempted to alter the terms to his own advantage, they stood firm and replied that unless the usual prices were paid they would not complete the order.

Others were less successful in maintaining their independence. In 1803 a William Hornby, junior, of Prescot, was making such things as drills, burnishers and other watchmakers' tools to the order of Stubs. These were sometimes brought to Warrington by a woman, who took back sums in part payment : when, on 1 April, 1805, Hornby sent goods to the value of £8 13s. $7\frac{1}{2}d.$ he wrote, " If you plase to let her ave £7 you will obledg." ; and on 9 August of the same year, in sending goods valued at £3 7s. 6d. he wrote, " if you'l ave the goodness to send mee by the Bot Coch today as I shall want it tonight Cash £3 0 0 you will very much oblg." Such urgency for payment suggests small resources ; and it was almost certainly lack of capital that led Hornby, some years later, to bind himself to work exclusively for the firm of Peter Stubs & Sons. By an agreement of 30 June, 1810, he contracted to deliver to John Stubs at his Warehouse in

[1] It is impossible to be certain about this, for there are occasional references to another Workmen's Book, which is missing.

Warrington such tools " well wrought and finished " as Stubs should order, " the wages for the workmanship whereof shall amount to the sum of Seven pounds ten shillings for each week of the said Term ". John Stubs, for his part, undertook " duly and regularly to settle and pay such prices and sums of money for the same as shall from time to time be customary and usual to be paid for such articles manufactured in the said County of Lancaster ". This meant that Hornby was to receive £7 10s. each week as wages for himself and his assistants, and that, at regular settlement periods, he was to receive a balance, out of which he would have to meet rent and other charges before realizing the net profits of manufacture. The agreement gives precision to arrangements which, as has been seen, existed informally with many outworkers. The merchant supplied the small master with much of his circulating capital, and, in return, obtained wares at an immediate price not exceeding prime costs. Later, when perhaps he had been paid for the goods, he handed over an additional amount to the manufacturer, who was thus reimbursed for the functions he exercised in providing fixed capital and controlling production.[1]

---

[1] A similar system existed in the works of Crowley & Millington at Winlaton. It was found at a later period in the salt industry : " Each head of a pan is paid 22s. weekly on account, and the balance is settled monthly, the work being appraised by the foreman of the salt works, who rejects or reduces the allowance for work in any way faulty or imperfect."—S. Timmins : *Birmingham and the Midland Hardware District* (1866), 142–3.

CHAPTER THREE

THE WORKERS—*contd.*

So far the story has been concerned with the relations between the file master and those of his workers who lived at some distance from Warrington. Several of these workers were men of semi-independent status, who perhaps combined manufacture with farming or other activities,[1] who themselves hired labour, and who provided their own workshops and tools, though not their own raw materials. There is evidence, however, that from the earliest days Stubs was also giving employment to a number of men either in his own premises at the *White Bear* or in workshops near by. Such were Benjamin Jolley, who spent much of his time in packing steel and sending it to the outworkers, and Edward Cranage, the nature of whose work does not appear, but who, on 27 September, 1792, entered into an agreement to work for Peter Stubs for eleven months " on the Terms he now does ". It is possible that both these men were paid regular weekly wages and were regarded as permanent servants ; but it is clear that most of the workers employed in Warrington, like those outside, were paid piece-rates. Occasional references in the Workmen's Book to another " Reckoning Book ", which is unfortunately missing, suggest that this was true of Thomas Griffith, Jacob Cooper, Joseph Ridgway, Peter Conway, Thomas Gad, Thomas Naylor and Robert Rockett, all of whom were employed by Stubs (but not all at the same time) during the years 1788–91.

Some of those whose names have been given above had been brought to Warrington from other places, and there is evidence throughout the records of persistent efforts on the part of Stubs to induce labour to move nearer to the headquarters of the concern. Skilled workers, however, showed extreme reluctance to leave their families or to transfer their homes to Warrington, and obstacles of all kinds were encountered. In September, 1792, Carolus Charles told Stubs he

[1] Of the makers of watch-tools and watch-pinions a writer of 1825 says : " Many of the manufacturers occupy small farms between Liverpool and Prescot and live with much comfort."—Smithers : *Liverpool, its Commerce, Statistics and Institutions*, 188.

believed he could find him a workman ; but a month later he had to confess disappointment :

I cou'd not light of the man. He was neither at his father's nor our Wakes but I went to him on Sunday last and he says his now Master got him senselessly drunk and hire'd him, tho' he told him if he ever hired him drunk it shou'd not stand, for he wou'd not be hire'd at all, nor has he stood to his first agreement which was to work at his own trade 4 days each week and he works at nothing but forging round wire, and he told me he would leave him. He is going tomorrow to his Father's to advise with him.

Difficulties presented themselves again in the following year when Stubs was trying to obtain an awl-blade maker and grinder : John Newby of Kendal wrote to say that it was impossible to find one there and that both men and goods in that business were very scarce ; and Eyre, Hall & Smith of Sheffield wrote to the same effect. Again, some years later, in 1797, when Stubs sought to enlist the services of his friends in Sheffield—this time to procure the labour of one or two file-forgers—Eyre, Hall & Smith replied to his letter as follows :

After having made enquiry we have since sent the Crier round saying that some file Forgers were wanted. Several have applied but when they knew who wanted them they none of them seemed willing to leave Sheffd. . . . On Monday we purpose sending the Crier round again. As the File Trade is not very brisk at present in Sheffield if you could make it convenient to come over you perhaps might meet with some that would answer your purpose as you then could inform them more particularly respecting Work &c. There are very few Workmen but what are in debt to their Masters (some of them very considerably) and by your being here you could judge if it would answer your purpose to lay the Money down for them.

On 28 March they informed Stubs that the use of the Crier had resulted in two applications, one from a man of 23 or 24 years of age, who asked for £9 in cash, the other from a youth of 18, who would accept three or four guineas, " but as he is under age there is no letting him have the money with any safety " ; and nearly two months later they were still urging that only by a personal visit to Sheffield could Stubs hope to satisfy his need.

One obvious method of overcoming the difficulty of obtaining adult skilled labour was to take boys and train them to the trade ; and Stubs seems to have made frequent endeavours to recruit youths from the surrounding districts. In 1792 Carolus Charles promised to do his best to procure a lad, but his efforts were frustrated : " The boy you mentioned in your last is dead," he wrote. " His bro' who was far advanced in his Apprenticeship together with his two sisters all died in a few weeks of a fever. I cou'd have plenty of others but none to do any good." Three years later, in 1795, the son of Edward Lancelot of Liverpool undertook to come to Warrington to work with Stubs ; but on 20 May the lad's mother wrote to say, " I hope you will excuse mee for not sending my son. The reason is I ad no shoes." And when this impediment had been surmounted and the boy was at work in Warrington there was opposition from the father, who wrote as follows :

July 1, '95.

SIR

Thom Lanslett was ingaged with a person to work in the Breefield for the Summer therefore I insist on your not keeping him—let him say what ever he will to you, as he has put the woman intirely out of the way—beside as a Father I insist on your sending him directly on your receiving this—or I shall take a method to bring him to me—so no more at present from yr Hubl. St.

EDWARD LANSLETT.

Apparently, however, the youth was satisfied with his employment and the father was obliged to give a reluctant consent to his remaining with Stubs :

July 7, '95.

SIR,

This lad of mine seems intirely bent on going to you but if you don't give him his washing, Lodging, Clothing & diet—or else allow him two shillings a week twoards his cloaths he must not remain with you so you w. let me know directly as I have much trouble about him—but if he continues with you you will be kind as to keep him much in the House as he is a very Masterefull Lad.

Yr. Hbl. St.

EDWARD LANSLETT.

The bringing of men and boys to Warrington from other places involved considerable cost to the employer : for example, in the case of Joseph Ridgway, to whom Stubs had to make advances " for coach and sundrys " as well as for the carriage of household goods. Men, moreover, sometimes remained in debt to those for whom they had previously worked, to shopkeepers, or to former landlords, and the new employer was expected to provide sums for repayment. Again, it was often necessary to find a workshop as well as a house for the newcomer : a receipt, dated 3 January, 1798, relates to the payment by Stubs of £2 10s. a year as rent of a workshop used by James Nicholson at Friar's Green ; and other receipts for 1800–2 show that £3 a year had to be found for the rent of a smithy occupied by

P. Watson in Old Road, Latchford. Nor was rent the only charge to be met if labour, once secured, was to be retained. In time of war men were liable to be withdrawn suddenly for military service : on 25 February, 1797, Stubs was called upon to pay £8 to one Roger Shanon " for to stand Substitute for Henry Naylor in the Supplementary Militia " ; and again in February, 1803, he had to find 7 guineas for a substitute for another workman, William Clough, who, however, repaid the amount by stoppages of 2s. a week from his earnings.   The records as a whole are, indeed, eloquent of the obstacles (familiar to students of the early factory system in the textile industries) confronting those who sought to draw scattered workers to a single place of employment and build up a homogeneous community of skilled labour.

In spite of all this, however, by the turn of the century Peter Stubs had made considerable progress towards his objective.   The advantages to him of the aggregation of labour are obvious enough.   So long as he had to rely on the services of outworkers spread over a wide area delays in the execution of orders were inevitable, specialization of labour to particular tasks was difficult, and damage might be done in carrying unhardened files from the place of manufacture to the warehouse.   In 1800 and 1801 customers sometimes complained of the quality of the files ; and, though the cause may have been the use of inferior steel (since supplies of the best were scarce at this time [1]), it is possible that supervision of work was becoming less efficient as the scale of operations increased.   If the business was to be properly conducted it was clearly necessary that a substantial part of the work should be done under the eye of the master himself.

For these reasons, therefore, Peter Stubs decided to construct workshops near his own home.   On 5 February, 1802, he obtained of Thomas Lyon of Warrington a lease for 500 years of a piece of land (1,931 square yards in extent) in what was then known as Cockhedge Fields, and which is now bounded on one side by Scotland Road. The rent was £15 a year, payable by two half-yearly instalments, and Stubs engaged within two years " to erect buildings of the yearly value of £30 at least, so that there shall always be found upon the premises tenantable buildings capable of producing more than double the rent reserved ".[2]   The workshops (some of which are still occupied by the firm) were erected shortly afterwards.   On one side of a cobbled yard were the forges, with the cutting-rooms above them,

---

[1] *Infra*, 45.

[2] The Indenture is in the custody of Messrs. Henry Greenall & Co., Solicitors, Warrington.

on another, the hardening and finishing shops, and on a third, the warehouse. The whole must have involved considerable expenditure, for receipts from the British Fire Office in 1806 show that the premises (which, however, possibly included the inn) were valued, for insurance purposes, at £1,900. The year 1802 thus marks an important stage in the evolution of Stubs from the older mercantile type, to the more modern type, of employer.

At the same time there is evidence of a clearer definition of the terms of employment. In the earlier years, it is true, craftsmen had sometimes bound themselves to work for fixed periods of time ; but, from 1800 onward, the number of written agreements increased, and the conditions became more specific. From at least as early as 1796 a Thomas Bashforth of Huyton had been forging file-blanks for Stubs [1] : by 1800 he had removed to Warrington, and on 29 January of that year he set his mark to a document binding himself to work for Stubs " on the Terms he now does for the space of two years from the date below or till such time he pays the money he now owes at two shillings per week, the said Peter Stubs having given him one shilling in earnest ". On the same day a similar bond was signed by another file-forger, Thomas Swindon, who also lived and worked in Warrington.

Three years later, when the new buildings were opened, many other workmen were bound. On 5 January, 1803, eight file-cutters [2] and one file-forger [3] undertook to work for two years " or till such time as we Respectively or Individually pay what we now owe or may owe to the said Peter Stubs or his assigns on the same terms as now do work " ; and on 4 February, 1804, ten other file-cutters [4] also contracted to work for two years " at the usual rate of wages or prices given and allowed to other workmen now in the present employment of the said Peter Stubs ". By binding only part of his labour force at any one time Stubs was adopting a practice common in the contemporary coal-mining industry ; it had the advantage to him that, since the bonds expired at different dates, it was never possible for

[1] On 22 September, 1796, he sent Stubs 66 dozen blanks, with a note saying, " I have whorked hup about half of the steel you sent me and I disire you will pay the carrige and deduct it from my account."

[2] James Pike, Thomas Boond, Richard Slater, James Taylor, Henry Taylor, Edward Rowland, Thomas Griffith and Benjamin Jolley, junior.

[3] Peter Hill.

[4] Edward Cranage, John Oldfield, Jonathan Cranage, Thomas Cook, Isaac Rowlinson, Joseph Ridgway, William Pearson, Henry Naylor, Thomas Potter, John Chaddock (or Chadwick). All signed their names, with the exception of Henry Naylor, who made his mark

all his workers to leave simultaneously or to make a concerted move to alter the conditions of work or payment.[1]

At the same time there is evidence that Stubs was meeting a considerable part of his need for labour by way of non-resident apprenticeship; for a bill presented by his lawyer for drawing up indentures shows that in 1803 no fewer than 22 boys entered into bonds to work for him.[2] The terms of engagement of one of these, William Metcalf, were probably representative. Metcalf was the son of a Warrington farrier; he was twelve years of age when he was bound to Stubs; and he undertook to serve at file-cutting for a period of seven years. His father agreed to provide " wearing apparel together with good wholesome and sufficient meat, drink, washing and lodging and also Doctors, Apothecaries and Nurses in cases of sickness "; and Stubs undertook to allow the boy a week's holiday at Christmas and to give him 1s. at the time of each Warrington fair. The wages were 2s. a week for the first year, 2s. 6d. for the second, and so on, until in the last year the apprentice was to receive 7s. a week. In 1804 indentures of a similar nature were entered into with other boys—with James Roscow, the son of a mariner; Robert Catteral, the son of a weaver, and William Forster, the son of a flatman: in each case the father belonged to Warrington and the boy continued to live at home.

By the end of the eighteenth century apprenticeship had lost much of its original justification as a system of technical and general training, and had become little more than a means of obtaining supplies of cheap, juvenile labour.[3] In the metal trades of most parts of England the custom had grown up for workmen, no less than for employers, to take apprentices; and there are some indications that this was so in the case of wage-earners employed by Stubs in Warrington. It seems likely, however, that before a workman entered into an indenture with a youth he had first to obtain the authority of his employer, and it is possible that some control was exercised over the conditions of work and pay of apprentices so bound. For when, in 1804, one of

---

[1] A Workmen's Day Book, 1802–4, makes it almost certain that all the nineteen men who signed these documents worked at Stubs' own shops. For, whereas in the case of others whose names appear in the book, a record was kept of the value of the work brought in and the sums paid out, in their case the only entries relate to money advanced and stoppages.

[2] The lawyer, P. Shuttleworth, charged 5s. for preparing each indenture and the stamp duty on each document was 15s. Altogether the legal and fiscal costs came to £25 6s.

[3] O. J. Dunlop: *English Apprenticeship and Child Labour*, 196.

Stubs' file-forgers, Thomas Swindon, engaged a boy to serve him for three years, the contract was witnessed by John Stubs and Joseph Wood, the one a partner and the other a traveller for the firm. Whatever may have been the evils of apprenticeship to employers those of apprenticeship to workmen far outweighed them. Peter Stubs and his sons were men of sensibility and humanity; and at a later stage in the history of the concern, when the harmful effects of the practice had become patent, they insisted that all apprentices should be bound to them directly and not to their employees—though elsewhere, in the file-making industry, workmen-bound apprenticeship appears to have increased, rather than to have declined, as time went on.[1]

In other parts of the country, notably in Sheffield, women were frequently employed in the trade : " 'Twas Jezebel's daughter I saw chopping files ", is the last line of one of Joseph Mather's best-known verses. But in the records of the firm of Peter Stubs references to the employment of women are surprisingly few. Among the outworkers, it is true, a wife sometimes continued to direct domestic production after the death of her husband ; and unmarried women or the wives of file-makers often acted as carriers or messengers for their men-folk. In Warrington itself, however, it would appear, no women were actually engaged in the file-making processes, though many of the wives and daughters of men who worked for Stubs found employment in the pin trade which flourished on the exploitation of infant labour in the town at this period.[2]

Unfortunately it is not possible to make a statement of the total number of workers employed by Peter Stubs at any point of his career. But that, in the later years at least, it must have been fairly large is clear from the amounts paid out in wages. For a period of five months from the beginning of February to the end of June, 1805, the wage-bill came to £2,386 6s. 3½d., which means that about £475 a month, or £5,700 a year, was at this time being paid to those employed by the concern. Wages were paid at irregular intervals when work was completed, and the records show that money might be distributed as often as ten times in the course of a single month. The largest amounts, as might be expected, were paid in Warrington

---

[1] In 1841, Thomas Cartwright, a file-cutter employed by the firm, told the Children's Employment Commissioners that all the children employed were apprentices to the masters, Messrs. Stubs.—*Children's Employment Commission. Appendix to Second Report, Part II*, m. 40.

[2] T. S. Ashton : " The Records of a Pin Manufactory, 1814–21 ", *Economica*, Vol. V, No. 15.

itself; but every week or so, John Stubs, or some other member of the firm, went over to Farnworth, near Widnes, to make payments to the outworkers, who probably left their shops and came to collect their earnings there.

Contracts entered into with particular workmen indicate that the rates of payment were the same as those made by other similar concerns in Lancashire. How these compared with wage-rates elsewhere is not known; but a letter from William Stubs, some years later, in 1814, shows that they were somewhat lower than those paid for work of the same nature by the file-masters of Sheffield.[1] Custom seems to have played a large part in the determination of earnings, and though it is possible that the workers sometimes took concerted action to obtain an increase, or resist a reduction of wages, no evidence has been found of any trade union among them. The masters, on the other hand, appear to have had clubs, or at least informal meetings. In one of the first of his account books, dated 1781, Peter Stubs kept a record of " Chapel Money ", which may have related to subscriptions to a professional society[2]; and a few years later, as will be seen, the larger employers in the file trade were holding conferences for the regulation of prices.[3] It seems probable that the arrangements for the fixing of prices were extended to cover that of wages; for in September, 1802, when the tool workers (who probably included the file workers) were standing out for increased earnings, a master manufacturer, Robert Roskell, of Liverpool, wrote Stubs as follows: " Have this day seen Mr. Green who told me he would write you this post respecting Tool makers. I think with you that a meeting is necessary and will in a few days again see Mr. Green and Messrs. Mather and Lascells and inform you the result." [4]

[1] " The prices of Sheffield Files herein ", he wrote, " are founded on the prices *offered* to the workmen but rejected by them. With the workmen's prices I shall be furnished before I leave. I find they are better paid in every branch than our men."

[2] Chapel Money in my hands which was due the 25 of March 1781   0 — 10 — 0
Chapel Money in my hands which was due the 25 of June, 4 of July   0 — 13 — 3
5 August   0 — 2 — 0
5 August   0 — 11 — 0

[3] *Infra*, 65–8.

[4] In the allied trade of nail-making, there is some evidence of attempts to keep wages at a common level. On 8 February, 1795, William Harrison & Son, a customer of Stubs in Chester, wrote " We shall be very much obliged if you can send us the present workman's prices of Nails in your Town and what they give there Masters for the Iron.

Although there is abundant information as to the rates of pay for different kinds of work it is not easy to determine the actual earnings of individual workmen. And even if these were ascertainable there would be the difficulty of deciding what deductions should be made to cover rent of the workshop, tools and fuel, where these were provided by the man himself, and what stoppages had been made in resp^ct of debts. A list of prices paid to workmen, printed in February, 1810, four years after the death of Peter Stubs, may serve, howevei, to give some indication of the level of wages of one class of workers. When they worked by time and not for piece-wages, the forgers received 1s. 6d. a day for making blanks of 9–11 inches in length, 1s. 4d. for making those of 12–14 inches, and 1s. 3d. for larger sizes ; and the corresponding daily wages of the strikers were 1s. 3d., 1s. 1d., and 1s. The cutters, apparently, were invariably paid by the piece, and it is unfortunately impossible to estimate their normal daily earnings.[1]

The regular work for regular wages, which were enjoyed by those employed in Warrington, as distinct from the scattered home-workers, might have been expected to confer a status of independence. But, from the earliest days, the Warrington cutters and forgers, like their fellows elsewhere, showed an inveterate tendency to call on their employer for loans, not only to meet unforeseen emergencies but also for current expenditure ; and it is difficult to imagine that debt did not spell poverty, at least intermittently. The following entries in

We keep a few nailers and have hear'd they are lower'd in price and want a letter with the prices that our men may see as our men work^d for the late Warrington prices." Some weeks later Harrison & Son thanked Stubs for his reply but said, " You sent us word of the price of Nails which you had from the workmen which I believe they told you wrong. If you cou^d enquire of some of the masters shall be oblig^d."

[1] The piece-rates paid for making cast-steel taper saw files were as follows :

Inches	Forger per gross s. d.	Cutter per dozen s. d.
1–4	2 4	9
4½	2 6	10
5	2 9	10½
5½	3 3	11
6	3 9	1 0
6½	4 6	1 1
7	5 3	1 2
7½	5 9	—
8	6 6	1 4

the first Workmen's Book may serve to exhibit some of the occasions of indebtedness.

Jacob Cooper Dr.

		£ s. d.
1789 April 18	To Cash at sundry times left in arear when settled for small beer	£1 4s. 3d.

Benjamin Jolley Dr.

1788 Sept. 13th	To Cash for Bedstocks	2	5	0
1790 Octr. 30th	To Cash lent to pay for your Cloaths	1	1	0

Thomas Gad Dr.

1790 June 26	To paid Mr. Thomas Skitt for Rent due to Mrs. Hind & an Ale score	3	8	4
Nov. 8	To Cash to your wife to pay your rent with	1	10	0

Even small sums of a shilling or so at a time were borrowed of the employer, and ale-scores at the *White Bear* figure largely in the accounts of the firm.[1] All such advances, great or small, had, of course, to be repaid by instalments of a few shillings a week, deducted from wages ; but since, before the first loan was extinguished a new one was almost invariably contracted, very seldom was the worker in a position of solvency. Many examples could be given, but the following will suffice. On 12 January, 1803, Benjamin Jolley, junior, borrowed £1 16s. ; within four months he had succeeded in repaying by weekly sums of one or two shillings, £1 3s. ; but on 21 May he borrowed a further 2 guineas, and on 20 August, by which time he had repaid £1 16s. more, he contracted yet another loan for £2 9s. 6d. On a single day, 19 November, 1803, stoppages were made from the earnings of no fewer than 29 workers ; and since the list includes the names of all but three of the men who had signed the bond of January, 1803, and of all the ten who were to sign that of February, 1804, it appears safe to say that indebtedness was the normal state of almost all who worked for Peter Stubs. One of the names in the list was that of Jonathan Cranage, who had formerly been a small

---

[1] A loose sheet, dated 1802, reads as follows :

Bashfoot to William Bibbey	0 – 5 – 0
Craneg to Beer	0 – 4 – 7½
William Boond lent Money	0 – 1 – 0
Henry Naylor lent Money	0 – 1 – 0
Do. Beer	0 – 6 – 9

master or outworker at Aughton, and whose debts, it may be surmised from the following letter, were the cause of his becoming a hired employee in Warrington.

February the 6 1796.

Sɪʀ   I am tould that you ar verrey Busey : If you ar I should be verrey glad to work for you.   If you will be so good as to lend me four or five pound I will come on Saturday and be hired to you and live in Warrington and you may stop so much a week from me.   Please to send it letter against wednesday to the Black horse and rainbow Liverpool to Jonathan Cranage file Cutter, Aughton.   That money would pay my debts and oblige your humble servant

JONATHAN CRANAGE.

For this man, as for all others to whom advances were made, there was kept a separate book, in which were set down, on the one side the amounts lent, and on the other the stoppages made against these.   Though they relate to a period somewhat later than that with which we are concerned the following entries, concluding the account of Cranage (with some caustic comments by John Stubs), may be taken as illustrating a very common state of affairs.

Jonathan Cranage

	Dr.	£	s.	d.		Cr.	£	s.	d.
1808					1808				
Jan. 23	To Bal. from O. Bk.	9	14	6	June 11	By 21 weeks stoppage 1/6	1	11	6
1809					1809				
Jan. 23	To 1 years rent	3	3	0	Jan. 23	By 33 weeks stoppage at 2/-	3	6	0
						By Balance	8	0	0
		£12	17	6			£12	17	6
1809									
Jan. 23	To Balance	8	0	0		By Profit	8	0	0
	This is the way to make a fortune					This is an unfortunate book and I am fearful its present Possessor will be no better than his predecessor.			

The " present Possessor " was James Ridgway, and John Stubs, it may be added, was not without good reason for his apprehension. For Ridgway had come to Warrington in 1802 from Birmingham, where he had worked for W. Whitmore & Son [1] ; and in January,

[1] Perhaps the William Whitmore of Newhall Street, described in *Pye's Birmingham Directory*, 1797, as a jobbing-smith.

1803, a letter from them had disclosed the situation at the end of his engagement there : " Our Late Servt James Ridgway stands indebted to us £13 - 9 - 10. If you by any means can do anything with him that the debt may be reduced we shall be much obliged."

It will perhaps be thought that the debtor-creditor relation between workman and employer was a temporary phase, originating in the loose arrangements for payment of earnings which were inevitable under the domestic system, and carried over to the early days of factory production. If so, it was a long time in dying. For a " Statement of the Workmen's Account " made on 31 December, 1810, shows that out of a total of 77 employees, 61 were indebted to their employers for an aggregate sum of £256 0s. 4½d. (one owing no less than £28 15s. 10¼d.) and only 16 were in credit for work done.

Nor was the concern of Peter Stubs exceptional in this respect. In Sheffield the " nickerpeckers ", or file-cutters, were similarly dependent on advances, and indebtedness forms the burden of Joseph Mather's celebrated doggerel, " The File Hewer's Lamentation " :[1]

> " Of slaving I am weary
> From June to January !
> To nature it's contrary—
>   This, I presume, is fact.
> Although without a stammer
> Our Nell exclaims I clam her
> I wield my six-pound hammer
>   'Till I am grown round-back'd.
>
> I'm debtor to a many,
> But cannot pay one penny ;
> Sure I've worse luck than any ;
>   My traps are marked for sale.
> My creditors may sue me,
> The bailiffs may pursue me,
>   And lock me up in jail.
>
> As negroes in Virginia,
> In Maryland or Guinea,
> Like them I must continue—
>   To be both bought and sold.
> While negro ships are filling
> I ne'er can save one shilling,
> And must,. which is more killing,
>   A pauper die when old."

---

[1] *The Songs of Joseph Mather, with Introduction and Notes by John Wilson*, 1862. Mather was born in 1737 and died in 1804.

At the works which Ambrose Crowley had established, a century earlier, near Newcastle-upon-Tyne there was the same story : the men entered into bonds for definite periods, and indebtedness to the concern began with the loan of tools and material. Crowley, or his son, had set up a court to deal with matters of dispute and to relieve cases of distress ; but the Minute Book for 1807 and succeeding years shows that much of the time was taken up in considering applications for loans and in laying down conditions for their repayment.[1] In the pin trade parents borrowed money on the security of the labour of children of very tender years.[2] In the silver-plate trade of Sheffield " the masters were continually enticing the workmen from each other's houses, giving them money to *hire* with them, and letting them get into debt as a kind of security ".[3] And among the nail-workers of Derbyshire, and the cutlers of Sheffield, according to a contemporary observer, borrowing was universal.[4]

It can hardly be held that the practice of making advances on the

[1] The Minute Book is in the Municipal Library, Newcastle-upon-Tyne.

[2] T. S. Ashton in *Economica, loc. cit.*

[3] *The Songs of Joseph Mather, Introduction* xvii.

[4] Farey : *The Agriculture of Derbyshire* (1817), III, 508 n.

" Under this system, the more considerable Master Nailers, have not been able to execute their orders, whenever trade was brisk, without allowing all their best hands *to draw Money on account on the Wednesday evening*, although frequently ' Saint Monday ', ' Saint Tuesday ', and even ' Saint Wednesday ' also had been religiously worshipped in the Ale-house, and few, if any, Nails had then been made, and when Saturday night came, a part only of the Wednesday advance could be set off without instantly losing the Man ; and the same again next week, and so on, until many of the best Nailers were 20£ in debt to their Masters : which debt, although not the least intention appeared of ever discharging it, was made the pretence, to any other Master who happened to have pressing orders for goods, to advance first Master's debt, and a Guinea or sometimes more to the Nailer in debt, to be spent in a good drunken bout, before he would lift a hammer towards executing such orders !

" The Cutlers of Sheffield, in Yorkshire, appear to have acted still further on this monstrous system, and nearly all the expert Journeymen were represented, to be thus held to their Master by debts, varying from 10£ to 50£ ; and that when different Masters received pressing or large orders for Cutlery at the same time, a sort of general bidding often took place among them, as to *who would advance or buy up the largest debt* to obtain a Man, and at the same time to increase it, by a fresh advance, and allow ample time for the *spending of the same*, without grumbling ! Ere this, the patent Nail-making Machines of security of future earnings was of benefit to the employer. True, it was one method of securing continuity of service and preventing workmen from transferring to other concerns. But only rarely was interest paid on loans made to workers ; bad debts were frequent ; and much time must have been wasted in keeping accounts of trivial sums borrowed and repaid by instalments. It is unnecessary to say that, to the worker, the practice was harmful and degrading in the extreme. For, as has been seen, it tended to immobilize labour, and it must have been a serious barrier to any effort to raise wages. Behind the employer there was often a court for the recovery of small debts, which could be used, not only to obtain repayment of sums advanced, but also for redress against workmen who returned insufficient work or were dilatory in executing orders.[1] If in other industries payment in truck or the " new discipline " must be given first place among the ills afflicting the wage-earner, in the metal-working trades indebtedness to the employer would seem to have been by far the most serious barrier to the attainment of economic liberty.

Birmingham introduced from America, and the alterations of the Apprentice Laws, have, I trust, in a considerable degree brought these Knights of the Hammer to reason. . . ."

[1] The records of the Warrington Court Baron for the Recovery of Small Debts are in the Municipal Library, Warrington. Unfortunately they cover only the period 1738–60.

CHAPTER FOUR

THE MATERIAL

THE small, high-grade files in which Stubs specialized were made from rods of cast steel supplied from Sheffield. This material, of peculiar hardness, was the product of three successive processes. First, bars of charcoal iron, imported from Sweden or Russia, were covered with fragments of charcoal, heated for several days in a cementation furnace, and so *converted* into steel. Next, the blister steel, so produced, was broken into small pieces and *refined* by melting in clay crucibles ; and lastly the ingots of cast steel were formed into rods of the required section by *tilting* them under the hammer at a forge.

The first of these processes—that of converting iron into steel—was a specialty of Newcastle, and blister steel was often spoken of as ' Newcastle steel '. From the early years of the eighteenth century, however, Swedish iron had been brought from Hull and turned into blister steel in Sheffield. But it was the discovery of the crucible process of refining by Benjamin Huntsman in the early seventeen-forties that laid the foundation of Sheffield's supremacy as a steel-making centre. His method was adopted by Samuel Walker of Masborough about 1749 ; by 1774 two other firms—Bolsover & Co. and John Marshall—had set up crucible furnaces ; and by 1787 there were, in Sheffield and district, eleven firms making cast steel, in addition to nine which confined their activities to the preliminary work of conversion.[1] The final process of tilting was a separate branch of the industry conducted by owners of tilt hammers, who derived their power from one or other of the streams with which Sheffield is intersected. As few of the refiners carried much stock, when an order was received they had first to smelt the steel and then make arrangements with the tilters ; and in times of drought or frost (which were not infrequent [2]) there might be a delay of weeks or months in delivering the rods to the customer.

[1] Gales and Martin : *A Directory of Sheffield,* 1787.
[2] Drought and frost are the subject of " The Grinders' Hardships ", a song probably written (it is said) by a member of the Grinders' Mis-

Many of the refiners were cutlers or tool makers who had begun to make steel for their own use and were now in a position to satisfy the requirements of others ; and some of them had become merchants or factors, trading, not only in steel and tools, but also in hardware, textiles and other commodities. Among those with whom Stubs had dealings were John Harrison & Son, Eyre, Hall & Smith, Jane Green & Sons, Harwood & Thomas, Shaw & Marshall, Love & Spear, Thomas Blake, James Cam, George Carr, Barber Genn & Co. and Joseph Hawksley. All, or nearly all, of these had evolved from the shops of domestic craftsmen. Jane Green & Sons and Shaw & Marshall had, apparently, begun as makers of edge-tools, Cam, Blake and Hawksley as file-makers, Barber Genn, Carr and Harrison as saw manufacturers.[1] In each case capital acquired in manufacture had overflowed into trade ; and, by the period with which we are concerned, small masters in the varied trades of Sheffield had come to be dependent on these firms for both raw materials and markets.

A striking feature of the relations between the small master and the factor was the almost complete elimination of payments in money. " We never pay any money for files in Sheffield," wrote John Harrison to Stubs on 7 September, 1801, " the makers taking steel etc. and would do more if we wanted." Harwood & Thomas went further : their warehouse was fitted with shelves and counters like an ordinary retailer's shop, and when cutlers and file-makers brought in the

fortune Society established in Sheffield in 1804.—*The Songs of Joseph Mather*, 112 n.

> " It happened in the year eighteen hundred and five
> From May-day to Christmas the season was quite dry,
> That all our oldest grinders such a time never knew,
> For there's few who brave the hardships that we poor grinders do.
>
> In summer time we can't work till water does appear
> And if this does not happen the season is severe :
> Then our fingers are numb'd by keen winter frosts or snow,
> And few can brave the hardships that we poor grinders do."

[1] The fortunes of the last of these, so it is said, had been laid by a Thomas Harrison who, taking to London one of his own workmen, sent him in his shirt sleeves to visit ironmongers' shops and ask for Harrison's saws. Then, a few days later, while the name was still fresh in the minds of the shopkeepers, Harrison himself called to solicit orders.—R. E. Leader : *Sheffield in the Eighteenth Century*, 107. The evolution of the other businesses mentioned is suggested by the headings under which their names appear in the Sheffield Directories of 1787 and 1797.

finished work, payment was made in a wide assortment of commodities. Receiving no money themselves, the small masters were unable to pay money wages to their workers : these had, therefore, to accept goods, or notes entitling them to goods, at the factor's store, and in this way barter in the wholesale trade resulted in the truck system in manufacture.[1]

Naturally, the Sheffield factors wished to adopt the same methods in their dealings with Peter Stubs : they were willing to take his files, but only if he would accept steel in return. No single factor, however, was able to offer an extensive market for files, and it was, no doubt, a desire to find as many channels as possible for the sale of his wares that led Stubs to distribute his orders for steel among so many firms. In the early days a large part of his requirements was met by two concerns, Harrison & Son and Love & Spear. But already in 1789 the first of these was complaining of a falling off of orders. " We seem to have lost you much in the steel way ", wrote Harrison in August of that year. " Tho' we deal with other file makers in your part for steel yet you have the whole of our orders for files and should be glad if we had more of you." There is evidence, however, that the balance was normally in favour of Harrison : in the year March, 1791–March, 1792, for example, he supplied steel valued at £143 6s. 3½d. and took files worth only £36 6s. 10d., thus leaving a substantial sum for Stubs to remit in money. When, therefore, on several occasions, he reproached Stubs for placing orders with other dealers there was an obvious retort.

In 1792, as an inducement to a larger business, Harrison conjured with the name of the inventor of the crucible process : " We have now got a very good Hand for making cast steel from Mr. Huntsman ", he wrote. " He says he can make it as good as Huntsman, and as we can try it as nere as any person in the saw way, we have found it very good. I have engag'd him for some years and find him a sober good workman." This man, Joshua Tingle, remained with Harrison till 1796. But in October of that year he informed Stubs that he had set up in business for himself, adding that he had done Mr. Harrison's entire work in cast steel for four years and had previously served Huntsman as sole superintendent in the same line for nine years and six months. " As I am now wholly upon my own Bottom," he wrote, " shall doubtlessly make as good an article as I can produce " : his terms were 58s. a cwt. " 'livered at Sheffield ". Since this price was no higher than that charged by other makers at the same time

[1] R. E. Leader, *op. cit.*, 110.

D

there must have been other reasons why Stubs declined the connection. Loyalty to Harrison was probably one of these ; but the fact that Tingle was not a merchant and could offer no outlet for files was possibly the determining consideration. Similarly with the Huntsmans themselves : they were specialists in steel-making and never became merchants or factors. Whether for this reason or because they asked a price substantially higher than that of other makers, Stubs bought no steel from them, except for one brief period in 1801 when it was difficult to obtain supplies of the best quality from any other source.

In order to secure their connection, the Sheffield factors sometimes insisted that the files they took should be made of their own steel : on 10 November, 1794, for example, Love & Spear sent a bundle of steel from Sheffield all the way by road (instead of part of the way by water) so that the files they had ordered might be made expeditiously and of their own material. Generally, however, there was no contract to this effect : the arrangement was merely that each party would do his best to further the trade of the other. Thus the association with Harwood & Thomas, which began in November, 1794, was the result of a letter in which they wrote : " We are in the habit of selling a good many Lancashire saw files which we have principally had from Liverpool, for which we have sent Cast Steel of good quality and charged at a fair market price. If it sute you to do business with us on these terms you will find us Customers worth your notice, our consumption being in the wholesale way."

The business that resulted was on a considerable scale. But if Stubs measured the benefits (as modern politicians measure the benefits of international trade) solely in terms of exports, he cannot have been wholly satisfied. For, to give an instance from later years, in the twenty months from December, 1804, to July, 1806, his sales to Harwood & Thomas were of a value of only £152, while his purchases from them totalled £680. It is possible, however, that the latter sum covered other goods as well as steel, for by this time Stubs himself had become a factor, trading in wares from Sheffield, among other things, on a fairly large scale.

Evidence of the debtor-creditor relation with other Sheffield businesses exists in abundance, but it would be tedious to set it down in detail.[1] Mention must be made, however, of two concerns which

---

[1] Two instances may be given here. On 15 January, 1805, James Cam wrote, " When your traveller was at my Warehouse last Journey, he promised that you would take files and cast steel for part or all of the amount of the order I show'd him provided it was executed by you.

supplied Stubs with steel without, apparently, buying files in return. The first of these was that of John Parkin, a man of humble origin, who had served as foreman to Love & Spear and was spoken of, in a letter to Stubs, as the best workman in England. He must have entered into partnership with Jonathan Hague sometime before 1787, for the firm of Hague & Parkin appears among the steel refiners in the Sheffield Directory of that year. From time to time, between 1790 and 1794, Hague & Parkin provided Stubs with steel, and all seemed well. But in 1793, a year unpropitious for industrial expansion, Parkin had set up a steam engine, no doubt to work a rolling and slitting mill, and it soon became clear that he had overreached himself. Rumours of financial difficulties are mentioned in a letter to Stubs from his daughter, Sarah, who was staying with the Parkins in the spring of 1794 ; and another ominous sign appeared shortly afterwards when Parkin began to offer steel at a special price, saying he had a large sum of money to raise. By this time Hague had sought safety by dissolving partnership ; and on 3 November, 1794, Parkin's son-in-law announced that his father-in-law had been arrested, that bail had been given, but that unless money was found within five days Parkin would be in jail. Three weeks later Jonathan Marshall wrote, " Mr. Parkin finding his engine too heavy a concern for him . . . had delivered all the keys to the Bank Compy. and another Compy. of whom he had the cast iron work &c." ; and a letter to the same effect came from Parkin himself.[1] Within a few months, however, Parkin had again begun business in cast steel. But he found himself hampered by lack of capital—" the more I do and the scarcer of money I am ", he wrote, and it is clear from his letters that he never recovered his former estate. From time to time Stubs sent him orders for steel, and the business connection, like the personal friendship, was broken only by death.

Very different was the career of the other industrialist, John Darwin.

Having now by me some very good Cast Steel I make you a Tender of any Quantity you may please to order at a Market price, and as we may in future deal with you I hope you will buy what you can of me " ; and on 7 May of the same year Wright Cocker & Co. wrote, " Please to give our steel a fair tryall and will give you orders for goods in Return as soon as we get them."

[1] The Banking Company was that of J. & W. Shore of Sheffield : it was to them that Stubs was required to pay over the balance he owed Parkin. On 21 May, 1795, they offered for auction the works Parkin had set up, with its newly erected engine, rolling and slitting mill, cast-steel foundry with 16 pots, and a cupola furnace for converting iron into steel. See notices in the *Iris*, 17 April, 1795, and succeeding weeks.

He, too, seems to have extended from steel-manufacture, not into merchanting, but into other branches of production. In 1795, attracted no doubt by the high price of iron resulting from the demand for munitions, he set up a blast-furnace ; and the fact that he supplied Stubs not only with steel but also with hammers, anvils, shears and other instruments suggests wide industrial interests. His correspondence shows that he shared with Peter Stubs a passion for horses : one letter, of October, 1792, refers to a visit to Doncaster races and another, of February, 1798, expresses the hope of meeting Stubs and his family at the Manchester race week " as usual ". In 1795 when Darwin joined the Sheffield Volunteers [1] it was Stubs who provided him with his charger—" a Gallant Horse ", which the public carrier refused to handle, so that Darwin had to come to Warrington for him and ride back to Sheffield, leading his own mare by the rein. On 17 April he wrote to announce his safe arrival home, adding triumphantly, " am this day in my Regimentals with Gun, Sword and Pistol and is going together to the Field of Exercise ". " The horse ", he wrote a few days later, " stands fire pretty well, tho' he had several times the first day like to have flung me both with firing and drawing swords." This was just at the time of his venture into iron-making : " Darwin ", wrote Jonathan Marshall in December, " has almost tired him out and looks very thin with soldiering and going almost every day to his Blast Furnace which has begun working about 10 days since." Neither arms nor horses, however, interfered seriously with Darwin's career : he became one of the leading industrialists in Sheffield, and was an original member of the association of ironmasters of Yorkshire and Derbyshire in 1799.[2]

Throughout, Stubs maintained very cordial relations with the Sheffield steel-makers. Orders and remittances to Eyre, Hall & Smith, to Love & Spear and to Hague & Parkin were frequently accompanied with a salmon, a box of sprats,[3] a goose or a hare. When Jonathan Marshall came to Warrington to solicit orders he sometimes took the opportunity of spending a day with the local anglers, and other steel factors occasionally brought their wives to visit the Stubs family. In return Stubs, now and then, sent one of his children to stay in Sheffield ; and a letter to her parents in June, 1794, when the sixteen-year-old Sarah Stubs had been sent as the

---

[1] The Sheffield Independent Volunteers came into being in April, 1794, under the command of the Earl of Effingham.

[2] T. S. Ashton : *Iron and Steel in the Industrial Revolution*, 178–81, and Appendix.

[3] Warrington was noted for salmon and sprats.

guest of John Parkin, shows the steel-makers as rivals, not only in trade, but also in hospitality : [1]

DEAR FATHER & MOTHER

I recived your letter on Monday the 26 of May and am glad to hear you are all well. I was at Mr. Smiths when I received your letter and as been there ever since. Mr. Smith said if I would not come and stop a week or two he would never come to our house again. I hade engaged my selfe to Mr. Spears but he wode make me come there first so Mr. & Mrs. Smith went to beg me of. Mr. Smith as made me a present of a Silver Fruit knife in a very handsom case. Mrs. Smith and me either go a visiting every day or else we have company. We was at Mr. Cams on day. He is a file maker. He desired me to give is Copts. to you. I have told Mr. Spear you want me to come home at Whitsuntide but he says he will hear nothing of it. Mifs Spear is reckoned to be one of the handsomest and Genteelest young Ladais in all Shefeild and keeps the genteelest company. They keep with pople that keeps their own caraige. You will think I have been wery extravagant but I am obleidged to apear as Genteel as ever I can or I should be nothing at all thought on. Mr. Smiths keeps the genteelest of company.

I just been haveing a tooth pulld out & my mouth is so painfule I can scare write. It is Bradfeild Feast next Sunday and Mr. Perkins says he will send a horse for me if I will com. Mr. Parkin receivd the salmon in good orderer and is very much obleidged to you for it. I have Dined at Mr. Harrisons latley. The mad very much on me and desired me to come any time. All your Freinds at Shefeild send there compts. to Mrs. Allen and love to my Brothers and Sisters

I am Dear Father & Mother
your Dutiful Daughter
SARAH STUBS.

In most of the Sheffield trades at this period prices were regulated by agreements among producers. The letters of the steel-manufacturers make no secret of the fact that the prices they charged were determined by collective action ; and there is evidence that the same was true of the charges made to them by the owners of tilts.[2] After announcing a small advance, due to the high cost of Swedish bar iron, in February, 1797, John Harrison added that " the present price was fix'd at a general meeting of the whole trade " ; and again in April, 1801, he mentioned that the price he was asking was that " adopted by the Trade ". Deviation from the agreed terms was rare. After the dissolution of the partnership of Hague & Parkin in 1794, John

[1] The Mr. Perkins referred to in the letter was the son-in-law of John Parkin.

[2] A printed list, dated 10 August, 1810, sets forth the prices agreed upon by a number of proprietors of tilts in Sheffield.

Parkin reduced his charges in order to counter tempting offers which Jonathan Hague had made to Stubs. But such price-cutting naturally gave rise to resentment : in December, 1796, Jonathan Marshall wrote to say that " at a meeting of the Cast Steel makers to agree about an advance on account of Iron being so much advanced, I was pointed out by your friend J. E. (John Eyre) for selling steel as no one could get a living at the price : it was giving it away as I had done to you ".

One method by which a producer could favour a customer without breaking his agreement with fellow-manufacturers was by varying the terms of credit. Normally, the custom of the trade was to allow six months and to deduct 5 per cent. from the invoice price if payment were made on delivery of the steel : these were the terms laid down by Jonathan Marshall, for example, in November, 1790, when he first entered into business relations with Stubs. But when, in June, 1791, payment became due for steel delivered the previous December, Stubs deducted the 5 per cent., in spite of a mildly worded protest that he ought not to take both time and discount. No single one of the Sheffield steel-makers, it would appear, was rigid in these matters : those who supplied Stubs with steel more or less regularly throughout the year accepted payment in December for the whole and allowed 5 per cent. on the running account. And postponement of payment did not, apparently, carry any penalty. When trade was depressed and money hard to come by early in 1794 John Harrison & Son wrote, " Respecting ye Bill you mention, would have you always make it convenient to yourself and particularly at these scarce times would not have you put yourself to the least inconveniency, we being not quite so near ruin as some Manufacturers may be from ye bad times " ; and in October, 1796, Jonathan Marshall said, " You don't need remitting me, would rather have an order." If a steel-maker was in need of funds the practice was not to press for payment but to induce it by increasing the discount : when Parkin was short of capital after setting up on his own account he allowed Stubs 10 per cent. for immediate payment.

As the war with the French increased in intensity and cost, rates of interest tended to rise and discounts were increased. In June, 1798, Eyre, Hall & Smith announced that in future they would add $2\frac{1}{2}$ per cent. to the usual 5 per cent., if remittance were made within one month of the date of invoice ; and when in December, 1802, the house of Longden, Binney, Todd & Co. began to supply Peter Stubs with steel, the terms they laid down were net cash for payment in six months, 5 per cent. discount for payment within three months, and $7\frac{1}{2}$ per cent. for a bill on receipt of invoice.

The price charged for steel varied with the quality and the breadth of the rods into which it was tilted, the smallest sizes being the most expensive. Stubs bought rods of varied sections, and when prices were increased he sometimes substituted a cheaper for a dearer grade of steel. For this reason, and because the invoices are not always explicit as to size and quality, it is not possible to give an exact statement of the course of prices. But the broad movements are clear enough. Between 1790 and 1796 the charge for a high-grade steel tilted into rods $\frac{1}{4}$ inch thick was 58s. to 60s. per cwt. In December, 1796, an increase occurred, and for nearly four years the price ranged from 60s. 8d. to 62s. 8d. In the autumn of 1799 another advance took place. For steel of the same size and quality 65s. 4d. was a typical price in the summer of 1800 ; by February, 1801, 70s. had been reached ; by April, 1801, 78s. ; and in the summer of that year Stubs was paying Harrison 80s., and Huntsman as much as 84s., per cwt. With the Peace of Amiens the price fell to 76s.–78s. ; but with the renewal of hostilities the upward course was resumed. In August, 1803, John Darwin accepted an order for $\frac{1}{4}$-inch steel at 82s., and delivered in June, 1804, at this figure, in spite of the fact that a further advance had occurred. During the rest of the year 1804 and throughout 1805 the usual price was from 84s. to 87s., though at one point, in 1804, 90s. was touched.

The movement outlined was partly due to well-known causes which led to a depreciation of British currency during these years. But there were special factors operating on the price of steel. At the end of 1796 the best Swedish bar iron, which for the previous four years had been selling at £16–£18 a ton, advanced in price to £22 15s.—a rise in which an increase of the British import duty played a minor part ; and by 1801 the embargo on exports of iron by Russia, and a further increase in the import duty, brought the price to £26 10s. From that point a fall occurred. During the Peace the expansion of imports caused prices to range about £20 ; and although the resumption of war and a further increase of import duties raised Swedish bars, towards the end of 1803, to £22 10s., the subsequent movement was again slightly downward.[1] The explanation lies in the fact that, by this time, steel made of British iron had so improved in quality as to be a satisfactory substitute, in many cases, for that made of Swedish and Russian iron. If the prices of cast steel supplied from Sheffield remained high this was due, no longer to an excessive cost of raw material, but to increased charges for converting and tilting.

[1] H. Scrivenor : *History of the Iron Trade*, 404, based on T. Tooke : *High and Low Prices* (1824).

As the difficulty of procuring foreign bar iron increased, after 1796, the Sheffield houses became more and more reluctant to supply cast steel to outsiders : such high-grade metal as they could obtain was required in the tool-making branches of their own businesses, and other cutlers and file-makers had to make shift with poorer steels.[1] From time to time Peter Stubs tried to meet his problem by sending his scraps to Sheffield to be remelted ; but the result was steel of an inferior quality, and it was not always easy to find smelters willing to undertake the work. Moreover, there were frequent delays in the process of tilting : during the greater part of the period there was severe pressure of work, and in times of drought only the orders of Sheffield men were executed. " It hath been an impossibility to get any steel tilted for several months back on acct. of the extraordinary scarcity of water ", wrote Joshua Shaw on 12 November, 1803. " The principal part of the Tilts are in the hands of File Makers and Cutlers in Compys. so that what little hath been done was mearly for their own use." In these circumstances it was natural that Stubs should look elsewhere for steel. At no time, however, did he sever his relations with Sheffield : as already remarked, the Sheffield factors were a valued channel for the disposal of his files, and in order to keep their custom he continued to give them orders for steel whenever they were able to execute them. A carriers' bill of 1804 shows that in a single period of two months (11 May–15 July) he bought from no fewer than seven of them, though by this time a considerable part of his requirements was being met from other sources.

The largest iron and steel works in the north of England at this period was that which had been set up by Samuel Walker and his brothers, in partnership with John Crawshaw at Masborough, near Rotherham,[2] about 1746. In 1787 the name of the firm appeared in the Sheffield Directory as Walker, Booth & Crawshaw ; but two years later Crawshaw left the business, and henceforth it was known as Walkers & Booth. Samuel Walker had been the first to copy the

---

[1] As early as January, 1798, according to a letter from Jonathan Marshall, the makers of the larger files were no longer able to use the best steel, and in November, 1799, John Harrison & Son wrote : " We have it in our power to send you as good steel at ye price as any of ye Sheffield people have, but it cannot be sent at ye present advance price by any of them, that you can depend of two parcels together being same Quallity or even both good, from ye great proportion of scraps they are oblig'd to use. (Best Barr Steel being now only 2/– per Cwt. lower than Cast Steel in ye Ing^t) and there being so much inferior Com^m Steel used in all branches of ye Sheffield Trades."

[2] For an account of the business see Ashton, *op. cit.*, 46–8.

methods of Benjamin Huntsman, and the making of crucible steel had played a large part in his business. In February, 1798, Stubs placed his first order at 58s. per cwt. As the price of steel in Sheffield rose Walkers & Booth increased their charge ; but generally their prices were slightly below those of their competitors ; and in a long letter of 14 November, 1799, John Harrison assured Stubs that he was following the right course in transferring his orders :

" There being so much inferior Comn. Steel used in all branches of ye Sheffield Trades, of course ye Scraps must be inferior likewise. On this acct. we are obligd. to use considerable mor Bar for Steel for our own use than we did being ye only way of having a certain article . . . Suppose you get good deal from Messrs. Walkers, Rotherham, and at their price you can't have so good anywhere in Sheffield, but I believe they are selling both lower than they could or would, only they are rather at Variance with some of ye Sheffield Houses and on that acct. do so, as their advance was not more than half that on ye Materials. However while they continue you cannot do better than with them. Ye Trade being now so small an object to us we both bye and tilt deal of their steel and if it was agreeable we should like to tilt some for you . . . Pretending to send good article at a price can't be afforded is only deceiving and may be great Injury to you."

In spite of the fact that the Rotherham concern could offer no market for his files Stubs found the connection a valuable one. His orders were for considerable quantities : in the last three months of 1799, for example, they amounted to £319 ; between 7 August and 14 November, 1801, to £483 ; and between 12 July and 11 September, 1802, to £538. Though Walkers & Booth announced, in the first instance, that their terms were six months' credit or 5 per cent. discount for ready money, in practice, like others, they were willing to allow the 5 per cent. when payment was made at the end of a considerable period. Between August, 1804, and June, 1805, they delivered steel, roughly once a month, to an aggregate value of £781 8s. 10d. : on 8 April Stubs made a first payment of £300, and when in August, 1805, he remitted the balance he was allowed the 5 per cent. on the whole sum.

During the years of shortage and mounting prices Stubs received many protests from his customers concerning the quality of his wares. " We have many complaints of your files lately being so soft that they will hardly whet a saw half thro' ", wrote Thomas Crane of Preston in August, 1799 ; and in the following July another customer, Thomas Dodds of Newcastle-upon-Tyne wrote, " Your files is not so good by ten per cent as they ware. Not so fine cut or yet so clear a temper, they have so dark and sooty look." It is likely that the fault lay in the inferior nature of the cast steel obtained from Sheffield, but there is another possible explanation. At this time Stubs was attempting to substitute shear steel for cast steel in the manufacture of the lower grades of files, and although quantities of this material were supplied by the Sheffield concerns, Newcastle was the principal centre of production. As early as 1794 Stubs was placing small orders with R. Beilby & Co. of Newcastle ; and in the following year he approached the concern of Crowley & Millington—the well-known enterprise which had been established by Ambrose Crowley at Swalwell at the end of the seventeenth century. They replied, however, that the rods he required were of too small a size for them to undertake, and that what they produced of this kind of steel was needed in their own works. Some years later, in 1799, Stubs wrote of his troubles to Isaac Cookson & Co. of Newcastle and Chester-le-Street, who advised the use of German or spur steel : " If you buy Cast Steel ", they wrote on 3 June, " no wonder that you meet with great Impositions as the generality of Manufacturers of that article are subject to be imposed on with scrap steel of very bad quality, some of it from Russia iron converted into Steel and sometimes steel very badly converted and often of two or three different Qualities that your files will often prove soft, others breaking in the teeth." The price they asked for double spur steel was 60s.–62s. according to the section of the rods, and the discount allowed was 1s. per cwt. for money, i.e. for a bill at not more than 40 days. Unfortunately Isaac Cookson & Co. had no tilt-hammer, and it was not possible for them to draw the steel into rods as small in section as was needed for the making of Lancashire files. It was, therefore, arranged that the bars should be sent to a tilter at Oughtibridge, near Sheffield. But the cost of carriage by Hull and Gainsborough was considerable ; and though Stubs continued to buy spur steel from Cookson, as well as from another Newcastle firm, Emerson, Milner & Co. (in 1805), his orders were never frequent or large. In 1804 he was buying steel of a James Wimble of Hull, and in the same year he obtained supplies from the brothers Hunt of the Brades Steel Works, Birmingham.

His attempts to find steel of proper quality at a price less than that prevailing in Sheffield and Rotherham brought Stubs into contact with one who was to play a distinguished part in the development of metallurgical science. At the turn of the century David Mushet was busy with his experiments in assaying and cementation ; and in November, 1800, he took out his patent for combining iron with carbon for the production of steel by the direct process. In 1801, along with others, Mushet erected the Calder Ironworks, near the site of which, in the same year, he found the Black Band ironstone which was to have such momentous consequences for the industrial development of Scotland. On 14 December, 1801, he and his partners sent Peter Stubs a small box containing specimens of the cast steel made and tilted at their works : they offered to supply any quantity at the prices current for cast steel in Sheffield, and added that " as carriage from Sheffield to your place is not less than 7 p. cent on the price of the steel [we] would make a difference to that amount in your favour ". Stubs found the new material somewhat soft for his purpose. On 12 February, 1802, the Calder partners, therefore, sent a second box containing steel which they thought would meet his needs and declared that " should it now be too hard or still too soft we can alter it ". " We make here ", they continued, " only Pig Iron and Cast Steel—the latter by a process entirely new, which enables us to make it with certainty of any given quality . . . Should you be in the way of supplying the spindle makers or other workers in cast steel we could furnish you with quantities . . . tilted to any sizes. Or should you be connected with any ffounders in your Country we should be happy to have their orders for Pig Iron at the Current prices pd. for that article of Scots manufacture." [1] Their terms were six months' credit " as Sheffield steel manufacturers ".

In April, Peter Stubs' son, John, then on a visit to Scotland, ordered a ton of Mushet's steel. This was shipped at Greenock for Liverpool, and several more tons followed by the same route. A number of letters from David Mushet express his concern to get the steel made exactly to Stubs' requirements ; and that some measure of success was attained is shown by the following letter :

CALDER IRON WORKS 2 *July* 1802.

Mr. P. STUBBS,
SIR,
We were duly favoured with your letter of the 21st ulto. ordering 7 Cw. Cast Steel.
Unfortunately our Tilter has been off work by fever for a month and still continues so weak as to be unfit for working. In this emergency we applied to a neighbour the only one in this country possessed of a tilt to make out your order. His mode of tilting however appeared so much inferior to our own and to that which you have been long accus-

---

[1] On 11 September, 1802, Mushet asked Stubs to supply him with the names of the principal consumers of steel in Manchester and for permission to refer them to Stubs for an opinion on the quality of his steel.

tomed to, that we stopt short and only finished the parcel noted in the annexed Invoice, which we have sent down to Greenock by land, that if it prove of service to you it may reach you as speedily as possible.

The moment our Tilter is able to work we shall inform you with a view of enabling you to regulate your orders without disappointment to yourself and proceed to finish your present order in a workmanlike manner.

It gave us great pleasure to hear that the quality of the steel gave satisfaction. We think you will find upon trial the parcel of No. 60 of which 3 Cw. were sent not much too soft for files.

We remain Sir

Your very Ob. servants

for the Calder Iron Co. & Self

DAVID MUSHET.

On 5 October, 1802, however, Mushet wrote to say he was "surprised and pained you find the steel soft", and in December he asked for the unsatisfactory material to be returned, saying he had now found out the cause of the trouble. Up to this time the price had been 70s. per cwt.; but in February, 1803, Mushet wrote to say that "in consequence of a rise upon ingots in Sheffield lately of £2 p. Ton" he had increased his own charge to 72s. Whether because of this advance, or (more probably) because of some continued imperfection of the steel, Stubs, apparently, gave no further orders. In 1805 Mushet severed his connections with the Calder ironworks. Many long years were to elapse before the methods of the science he did so much to create replaced the traditional skill of the Sheffield worker in the production of high-grade steel.[1]

[1] It would be profitless to describe at length the sources from which Stubs obtained materials and equipment, other than steel. Coal and coke were supplied regularly by James Orrell & Co., Thos. West & Co. and other local colliery concerns. Salt, used in the hardening process, was bought of Alice Hesketh of Warrington; oil for the whetstones, and for treating the files before packing, of George Crosfield and Silvanus Chandley; oak for hammer shafts, and poplar for file handles, of Edward Black and Peter Lythgoe; paper for wrapping the files of Thomas Greaves of Mill Bank; and timber for making the boxes in which the files were packed of a variety of local landowners. Anvils were obtained of Cockshutt & Armitage of Mousehole Forge, near Sheffield, as well as of John Darwin; oil stones of John Moseley of Covent Garden; marks for the stamping of initials on the files of Richard Bayley & Co. of Sheffield; bellows and vices of Jonathan Holland and John Povey of Warrington; grates, fire-shovels, tongs and other ironwork of Caldwell & Whitley of the Bridge Foundry, Warrington; and candles of Thomas Watt, also of Warrington. Local bricklayers were frequently employed on repairs at the forges and smithies, and a number of woodworkers were kept in more or less regular work, at piece wages, in making boxes.

CHAPTER FIVE

THE MARKET

I

In the early years of his enterprise Peter Stubs disposed of the larger part of his output through wholesale ironmongers or factors. The position of Ashton-in-Makerfield in the geographical centre of the metal-working district of south-west Lancashire led to a concentration of dealers in this relatively small town ; and it was from such concerns as those of Chorley & Peet, Clowes & Whitley, Clough & McGuffog, and William Harris that the bulk of the orders for files was at first received. All of these firms seem to have combined wholesale trading with manufacture. The invoice-heading of Clowes & Whitley, for example, describes the partners as " Manufacturers of all kinds of Iron Hinges, Locks, Nails, Thumb Latches, Wood Screws, Bed Screws, Smiths' Vices, Spring and Round Bolts, Chains, Backbands and Traces, Hoes and Bills, Axes and Adzes " : it is eloquent of the diversity of products of the Lancashire industry at this period. Files, it will be noticed, are not mentioned ; but it is probable that other of the Ashton ironmongers included them among their products ; for in January, 1790 (evidently in reply to a protest from Stubs), Chorley & Peet wrote to say, " We shall not meddle ourselves any more with manufacturing, therefore we hope you will not allow any further discounts to any person so as to undersell us and that everything may remain as at first."

The scale of dealings with the Ashton ironmongers may be indicated by a single instance : between May, 1791, and April, 1793, Clowes & Whitley received of Stubs files valued at £462 11s. 7¼d. The orders frequently came in the form in which they had been received by the factors ; and Stubs had sometimes to make up as many as forty separate packets of assorted files, each ready for the particular customer. In no case, however, was the name of the customer mentioned ; and when, to save themselves the trouble of copying, Clowes & Whitley sent the original letter containing the order, they were careful to cut out the name and address, lest Stubs should be in a position to enter into direct relations.

Nevertheless it was inevitable that some knowledge of the market should come to the ears of the file-manufacturer ; and sometimes the initiative came from the client of the Ashton firm. As early as 1789 Chorley & Peet found themselves reluctantly obliged to give an introduction to the firm of Warham, Potts & Smith of Leeds, who described themselves as " Factors and Wholesale Ironmongers, Manufacturers of Hair Seating, Curl'd Hair, Nails, Sprigs, fine Locks etc." [1] " Herewith is Mr. Warham ", they wrote, " who wants to know the prices of files. You must tell him that the lowest price is 1s. p. Inch p. doz. and 12½ p.c. Disct. He will try you a good deal for more. But don't let him have it." It was the opening of a long and profitable association for both parties. Sometime in the 'eighties Stubs began to make use of the services of two factors—Samuel Royle and Atherton & Hewitt—whose headquarters were at Wigan. As early as 1782 files made by him were sent to London on the instruction of a Peter Atherton ; and a few years later large orders were received from London in the name of Atherton & Hewitt, who probably had a warehouse there. Others in the metropolis who bought direct were James Rawlins of Clerkenwell, Thomas Jackson of Smithfield, and Walker & Beck, who, in 1796, asked that the files should be stamped with their own initials, instead of with those of Stubs. Rawlins, and Walker & Beck, were wholesale dealers and part of their business (like that of John Crompton who opened an account in 1802) was overseas. In 1801 a Henry Atkinson asked to be allowed to sell files in London on commission, offering the security of landed property in Lancashire and Yorkshire for any stock that might be entrusted to him. There is no evidence, however, that Stubs ever made use of commission agents, though after his death his successors conducted foreign sales in this way.

Yet another factor, trade with whom led to a wide connection, was Abraham Chamberlain of Skipton. Situated, as it was, at the junction of the highroad from Lancaster to York with that from London to Richmond and beyond, Skipton was well placed to serve as a distributing centre ; and, after 1796, the Leeds and Liverpool canal gave cheap communication with important industrial areas. From here Chamberlain made extensive journeys : orders from him, sent when on the road, reached Stubs from various parts of the North Riding, Westmorland and the southern counties of Scotland. The trade was highly competitive. " You may send us 200 doz. files ($3\frac{1}{2}$–$5\frac{1}{2}$ ins.) ",

---

[1] Warham, Potts & Smith had also an establishment in Birmingham. Pye's *Birmingham Directory* for 1797 describes them as Merchants of Russell Street.

Chamberlain wrote in May, 1792, " if you charge the same terms you do the Ashton factors. We expect no better—we shall not be satisfied with worse." And in giving an order for 397 dozen files in September of the following year, he remarked that he had been obliged to sell a previous consignment at prices lower than usual " as two other houses who carry your files had done the same ". Competition apart, it was to the interest of the factor that the final price should be kept low, so as to induce a large volume of sales : " Not a dozen of your sort of files has been bought since you made the advance", said a letter of 3 June, 1791. Again in February, 1793, Chamberlain was urging lower charges : " As there seems to be a general reduction of Wages about to take place in most Parts of the Kingdom," he wrote, " your File Cutters we shou'd suppose will be among the rest."

Chamberlain deeply resented any intrusion of Stubs into the market of the area in which he travelled. " We think it necessary to observe ", he remarked early in 1793, " that if you apply yourself for Orders in Yorkshire we must make a fresh Connexion. The bad effects of your Journey some years ago [were] felt a long while afterwards." A few months later he wrote indignantly, " We beg to know on what terms you have been selling Files to the retail shops in Leeds and other places in Yorkshire and on what terms you mean to supply us in future. . . . It will not do for us to travel for orders for you when you will serve Shops, our Customers, on same Terms." Overtures from shopkeepers, he insisted, should be repulsed. " Shou'd any of our friends hereabouts write you themselves you should refer them back again ", he advised in January, 1794 ; and in October he expressed suspicion that some of his customers in Darlington had discovered the name and address of Stubs and would be applying for files themselves. Yet again, in February, 1795, he wrote, " It is we trust unnecessary to repeat that you will not interfere with us any further in the sale of your files in this part." But by September of the same year he had to admit defeat : " from a journey we have just been at York find all our friends now apply to you themselves from that Quarter ". Nevertheless, he must have retained custom in other places, for at the opening of the new season he told Stubs he hoped to be a good customer in 1796 " if you do not steal away any fresh shop from us ".

Among the ironmongers whose custom Stubs obtained with the unwilling aid of the Ashton, Wigan, or Skipton factors were John Wilkinson of Leeds, Braithwaite & Backhouse and T. & J. Newby of Kendal, Thomas Milner of Newcastle-upon-Tyne, and a number of Glasgow houses, including those of William Johnstone, Archibald Turner, James Sword, Auchie & Co., A. & W. Coats, and Sorley &

Stirling. In opening accounts with Stubs several of these promised secrecy : in March, 1793, Archibald Turner promised that if he were allowed 10 per cent. discount no one should hear of it, and in the same month Sorley & Stirling wrote, " You may depend that none of the Ashton folks shall know so much as that we are dealing with you retail only."

New trading connections were also opened up through the medium of those who supplied the raw materials. In the beginning, Stubs obtained his steel from the Ashton houses ; and, after 1794, when Abraham Chamberlain set up a furnace, supplies sometimes reached him from Skipton. But, as has been seen, Sheffield was the main source, and there was an understanding that the Sheffield factors would do their best to extend the sale of the *P.S.* files. Just as the association with the Lancashire factors led to trade with ironmongers in the North and in London, so that with Sheffield led to the opening of accounts in the Midlands and the South-west. In June, 1790, a letter reached Stubs through the post with the following superscription, " Please to deliver this to the File Maker and Publican who Marks them S.P. [*sic*] Warrington, Lancs." It was from Thomas Richardson of Birmingham, who afterwards claimed that he had been the first retailer in the town to stock files of Stubs' make, and who had previously bought them through a Sheffield factor.[1] Again in 1790 trade was established with Joseph Tarratt of Wolverhampton and with Samuel Timmins of Birmingham [2] ; and in 1792 (through dealings with the second of these) an account was opened with James Dowell of Bristol, who sold large numbers of files, not only locally, but also overseas. Another client whose custom Stubs obtained through his connection with Sheffield was Charles Homer of Nottingham. On 15 April, 1793, John Harrison & Son wrote, " One Homer of Nottingham has been used to have some of your files from us, and he proposes writing to you of himself. If he should, think you need not allow any discount to him. You'll please take notice of this has he his a pretty good customer to us for our articles."

Enough has been said to indicate the part played by the factor in the development of the commercial side of the file-making concern. From the start Stubs had direct dealings with retailers in Lancashire and Cheshire ; and, gradually, ironmongers in places more distant from Warrington found it possible to dispense with the services of middlemen. One satisfied customer after another told his friends of

---

[1] His address was No. 5 Bull Ring.

[2] Pye's *Birmingham Directory* for 1797 describes Samuel Timmins as a Factor of Bromsgrove Street.

the merits of Stubs' files. In 1790 an engineer to Robert Peel, the cotton-spinner, gave an introduction to Thomas Cave & Co., retailers of Barnstaple ; in 1793 Richard Jones, a sawyer of Chester, introduced another shopkeeper, Thomas Morris of Ruabon ; and so on. By the middle of the 'nineties, if not earlier, it is probable that direct sales to retailers exceeded those made through intermediaries.

Besides the retail ironmonger's shop there were other channels for the disposal of files to the ultimate purchaser. The local fair still played an important part in the economic system, as a means of supplying commodities of all kinds to the working classes. In September, 1790, Thomas Richardson of Birmingham asked that his order should be delivered in time for the fair that was to open on the 29th of that month ; and in May, 1794, he asked for files to be sent by coach, instead of by waggon, so that they might arrive in time for the fair on 12th June. (" I will pay for them ", he added optimistically, " when the Warr be over.") In September, 1793, Thomas Jones, and in September, 1794, Thomas Ellis, requested that supplies should reach them before the Chester fair on 10 October. And in 1805 James Dowell of Bristol and C. E. Badger of Nottingham both gave special orders for files to be disposed of at local fairs. The fair was the occasion of an annual holiday ; men who were out of work visited it in the hope of meeting employers who were in search of labour ; and it must have provided the semi-independent craftsmen with a useful opportunity of replenishing their stocks of tools.

Another institution which served similar functions was the public-house ; and in the case of Peter Stubs there were special reasons why it should be used as a means of extending trade. For besides making files Stubs was a brewer of excellent ales, which he supplied to other innkeepers in the neighbouring parts of Lancashire. It was natural that he should utilize the trading connections so established to extend his main business ; and in Manchester, in particular, the tavern afforded a by-no-means unimportant outlet for the disposal of files and tools. In November, 1789, John Brown of the *Nag's Head* in Jackson's Row sent an order [1] ; in March, 1793, James Kekwick, proprietor of the *Royal Oak* in Deansgate, wrote, " There is a many Sawyers and Joiners that frequent my house been at mee for some time past to write to you for files, knowing I come from Warrington " ; and others who made occasional purchases were John Harrop of the *Blue Bell Inn*, in High Street, and Michael Hunt of the *Legs of Man* in Gravel Lane, Salford.

[1] The inn is still in Jackson's Row : it is now known as the *Old Nag's Head.*

Whether sales were effected through factors, through retailers, or direct to customers depended largely on the terms of credit. In all cases the files were invoiced at prices set down in lists drawn up by Stubs, sometimes in concert with other Lancashire manufacturers. But a trade discount was always given to the larger purchasers, and a further allowance was made for prompt payment. In the case of the factors the trade discount was perhaps 15 or 20 per cent. on files and 10 per cent. on other tools : " We are to sell at the same price as you would ", wrote Abraham Chamberlain in 1790, referring to tools, " and we expect 10 per cent. for our trouble and hazard." In addition, long terms of credit were extended to the factors ; payment was made, not at regular intervals, but intermittently at the convenience of the factor, and Stubs had often to wait months or even years for his money. To the Sheffield factors who took files in part payment for steel the terms were less generous ; no doubt they were considered to draw the bulk of their profit from the sale of steel ; on files they usually obtained only 5 per cent., and sometimes not even this.[1]   Traders in Birmingham, on the other hand, generally received 10 per cent. and 6 months' credit.   These were the terms asked by Thomas Richardson, who told Stubs in 1792 that he was allowed them by the Sheffield file-makers ; and that they were granted to others also is shown by a note in Stubs' hand, " promis'd to allow 10 pr. ct. on Clock and Watch, 5 on saw files, if wholesale 6 mos. Cr." made at the foot of a letter from John Solomon & Co. of Birmingham [2] in 1794.   Dealers in London were even more favoured : they always claimed, and obtained, 15 per cent. discount ; and, in addition, the manufacturer had to pay carriage.

Differential treatment of this kind led to demands for better terms from merchants in the less-favoured markets. In announcing, in 1805, that he had moved his business to Northampton, a wholesaler, Z. Rowton, told Stubs that he would henceforth expect his goods to be sent carriage paid, as to London houses, " for if I do not buy as they do, I cannot sell so ".   Again, in the same year, a Quaker wholesaler of Sheffield, Richard Walton, protested that he had been allowed only 5 per cent., though both Peter Stubs and his son had promised

---

[1] On 29 May, 1797, Jonathan Marshall, of Shaw & Marshall, wrote, " Your 1st Invoice of Files says you would allow 5 p. Cent which Mr. Shaw says is all the profits he can get from them."   But in the following year, after Shaw had sold the files at Stubs' own price, with 12 months' credit, he found that the file-maker was unwilling to allow the discount— probably because he had had to wait so long for payment.

[2] Described in Pye's *Birmingham Directory* for 1797 as Dealers in Watch Materials, Dudley Street.

10 per cent. with a running account of 12 months, " which is only
equal to 6 mo. on every parsell ". After a long correspondence, in
the course of which Walton pointed out that he had sold more than
£300 worth of files on the expectation of these terms, a compromise
was effected : Walton was to have a running account of six months
with 10 per cent. discount. When James Dowell of Bristol began to
trade with Stubs in 1792 he asked for 10 per cent. and twelve months'
running account, saying that these were the terms he had been accustomed to from the Liverpool firms with whom he had previously done
business. Stubs was willing to concede the running account but would
not give more than 5 per cent. ; and for twelve years Dowell had to
be content with these terms. In 1805, however, when he was doing a
substantial trade, he protested vigorously against treatment which
seemed to cast reflections not only on himself but also on his native
town : " I have heard ", he wrote, " that you allow 15% off your tools
in London, and your son admits that you allow 10% off files with Credit
in Birmingham . . . Bristol is thought to be equal to any Port or
Place of England. It is ye Key to ye West of England and S. Wales."
When a trader failed to pay at the time stipulated he was charged
interest. In January, 1804, Warham, Potts & Smith of Leeds, who
had a twelve-months' running account, wrote : " We acknowledge we
have taken rather longer credit than perhaps you give to every one but
at same time we pay'd you £12 – 11s. – od. for it, which is 5 pr. ct.
upon the whole of last year's Acc^t, & which is the same Terms we
understand some of your Customers have to whome you give 6 Mo.
Credit."

Small retailers were usually given no discount ; though 5 per cent.,
or more, was sometimes allowed to regular customers : 5 per cent. at
6 months was the arrangement with B. Hobson of York in 1795, and
7½ per cent., for payment within three months, with L. Tipper of
Cheadle in the same year. In January, 1799, R. Lloyd of Shrewsbury
wrote, " I recollect you mention'd you cou'd not allow the dist. unless
immediately paid for. *That* rather surprises me, as I *know* you do
it to others at 12 months. Therefore I think myself entitled to the
same, except that my sale may not be quite so large. I have still
further to observe, I can have 5 p. c. Dist. of *your own files* from
another person and 6 months' Credit. Therefore think it extremely
odd you shou'd say anything of allowing me the Dist." Lloyd,
however, was not prompt in his payments : in each of the two preceding years he had failed to remit at the end of the twelve-month
period, and his total purchases were less than £10 a year. When a
retailer bought on a larger scale and was regular in remitting, Stubs

was willing to make concessions. The Scottish shopkeepers, in particular, were prompt payers. In March, 1793, Archibald Turner of Glasgow asked for 10 per cent. for payment within one month, and Sorley & Stirling for 20 per cent. for immediate payment. And in 1805 Walter Miller of Perth informed Stubs that he had deducted 10 per cent. " which I understand you allow for money payment, 5% off account and 5% for cash ". " Mr. John Whitley ", he added, " serves us at the same prices and 9 or 12 months' credit, which he could not do if 10 p. c. were not allowed."

At this period the line of demarcation between wholesaler and retailer was not easy to draw : many of Stubs' customers traded in both ways, and arrangements made with one trader were often a cause of offence to others in the same district. In 1794 Archibald Turner of Glasgow wrote, " You allow Sword and Co. 10%. You should allow it me." In 1797 J. Newton of Newark complained that Birmingham riders or factors were able to sell *P.S.* files in Lincoln at a lower price than he could : he therefore asked for more liberal terms. The following year John Wilkinson of Leeds wrote, " I am informed by a traveller that you allow 15 p. Cent. I have only taken off 10 p. c. I think you ought to do as well for me as any other, as I have most of them to sell by wholesale." It must have required much diplomacy, and a nice adjustment of rates of discount, to preserve trade where so many separate interests were in conflict. The records, indeed, afford an interesting field of realistic study in the tactics of what theoretical economists now call monopolistic competition.

The tendency to eliminate the middleman was a marked feature of trade at this period, for improvements in the means of communication and in facilities for the spread of trade information were reducing the need for his services.[1] Increasingly, Stubs spent more of his time in travelling and less at headquarters in Warrington. After 1799 his son John acted as a rider-out, and in 1802 the services of a traveller, Joseph Wood (who subsequently became a partner in the firm) helped to extend the range of custom and to ensure more prompt payment of accounts. By personal visits it was possible to ascertain exactly what rate of discount it was necessary to concede in order to draw away from the factors the trade of each customer. In the early years such encroachment on the province of the middleman had aroused bitter resentment ; but as time went on the attitude of the factors became one of resignation. When Stubs opened an account with McAdam & Patterson of Belfast, Chorley & Peet, who had previously had this trade, merely asked him " to take Robert Patterson's Files to your

[1] See Westerfield : *The Middleman in English Business.*

own acct., he being Partner with Jas. Mc.Adam who buys files from P.S. cheaper than we do ".

From as early as 1790 references in letters from Liverpool to the necessity of delivery before the sailing of ships suggest that files and tools supplied by Stubs were being sent overseas. As, however, coastwise trade was important at this time it is possible that these shipments were for other parts of Britain. But by 1796 it is clear that a substantial trade in the *P.S.* files was being done in the American market. The brother of a Warrington doctor named Jackson had entered into partnership with one Barlow of Stockport, whose father (as a correspondent told Stubs) was " doing very well in the cotton trade and has got a very pretty property by it ". Jackson & Barlow were evidently general merchants, engaged in foreign trade ; and a Thomas Carter, who had been sent as their agent to America, was seeking to establish a trade in Stubs' files there. " Please to forward per Ship Hope an Invoice of hand-saw files amount about £40 ", he wrote on 14 June, 1796. " No other sort answer so well here. They complain about the price but we recommend them as first quality, and hope we shall be able to sell a considerable quantity when they come to be tried." He asked also for about the same amount of clock-makers' files and added that the *Hope* would sail in less than a month after the receipt of his letter.

About the same time files of Stubs' make were reaching the United States through other channels : in January, 1796, Waldo Francis & Co. of Birmingham [1] ordered assorted files " as usually sent to America " ; in May, Jonathan Hoyland, a Quaker merchant of Sheffield, ordered clock- and watch-makers' files for the same market ; and in July, 1797, Thomas Kirkup of Sunderland mentioned that the files he had ordered were for South Carolina. Among other merchant houses which, in succeeding years, bought *P.S.* files for sale in America were those of James Dowell of Bristol, Warham Potts & Co. of Leeds and Hamilton, Maher & Co. of Liverpool.

There is evidence that some of the files sent by Stubs to London were for the West Indies : James Rawlins, who was a customer for many years, did a large trade with Jamaica. In December, 1805, Joseph Tarratt of Wolverhampton ordered gun-smiths' vices and gold and silver wire-drawing plates for the East Indies ; but no other instance has been found of files going to the Far East. With Europe, trade was made difficult by war and diplomatic friction. In February, 1797,

---

[1] Pye's *Birmingham Directory* for 1790 describes them as Merchants, and gives the address as Brittle Street : in the *Directory* for 1797 the address is Moon Street.

James Cam of Sheffield, who had connections with various parts of the Continent, wrote to say that entry of English goods into Sweden was prohibited and that he would be glad if Stubs would take back the goods he had delivered.   But in the brief interval of peace between October, 1801, and May, 1803, there was a brisk sale.   In June, 1802, William Worrall of Liverpool mentioned that he had sent Stubs' book of patterns to Hamburg and that he expected some good commissions ; and in the same month Backhouse & Robinson of Liverpool wrote to say that they were receiving enquiries from the German market.   Some of the trade survived the renewal of hostilities : James Cam was giving orders for files in 1804, and for " pin-engines " in 1805, for St. Petersburg.[1]

It is not possible to estimate the relative importance of the home and foreign markets in the economy of Peter Stubs : all one can say is that much the greater part of his business was in Britain ; and that though his successors extended the policy of direct dealing to foreign sales, in the period covered by this study the firm was not yet in a position to dispense with the services of the specialized export merchant.   To have effected a virtual elimination of the wholesaler in the home trade was, after all, quite sufficient achievement for the first generation of a business of this character.

II

It is not easy for the layman of to-day to appreciate the part played by the file in the manufacturing processes of earlier generations. Modern methods of moulding, stamping and pressing, the development of the lathe and the emery wheel, and the production of standardized parts by machinery, have all served to reduce the need for it.[2]   Peter Stubs belonged to the age of the hand-tool, rather than to that of the

---

[1] An attempt to carry *P.S.* files to France is mentioned in a letter from Stubs' traveller Joseph Wood, sent from Manchester on 13 January, 1803 : " Mr. Costigin the Machine Maker has made his exit into France.   I was out after that concern till 12 o'Clock last night and at last I secur'd the Box of Files which was to have followed him to France this W^k."

[2] Perhaps the milling machine and the grinding machine did most to replace the file.   The great increase in the use of press tools for modern repetition work has given a remarkable impetus to the file industry ; there is a large amount of filing work in the process of die-making especially.   It is nearly all machine filing, however, and it is an interesting comment on the superiority of hand-cut files that the principal makers of filing machines to-day obtain their files from the only remaining hand-cutters in England.

machine : in the days when he was building up his business there were few workers in metal, wood, stone, leather or textiles who could dispense with the file.[1] So far attention has been given only to the channels through which sales were effected : a brief account must now be given of the ultimate sources of demand.

The first recorded order, which came from William Barrow of Prescot in 1777, was for files to be used by the makers of watches and clocks. It was followed by many others from both Prescot and Liverpool ; and by 1790 watch-makers' files were being supplied to dealers in Wigan, Preston, Sheffield, Grantham and other towns. In 1792 Stubs obtained a first introduction to Coventry, and two years' later the manager of the shop of Susannah Stephens promised to get the files into use at a large manufactory of watches there, asking, however, that Stubs should have no dealings in Coventry except through him. At the same time London and Kendal had become important markets, and, as has been seen, quantities of clock and watch files were subsequently sent overseas through merchants of Bristol as well as through those of London and Liverpool.

Small, finely-cut files, similar to the ones used by watch-makers, were provided for workers in a wide variety of the lighter trades—for goldsmiths in London, ivory-comb makers at Chester and Preston and pin-makers (employed by Sir Robert Peel) at Radcliffe and Blackburn. A maker of fish-hooks at Kendal and a manufacturer of gun-locks and pistols at Wednesbury were among the specialized craftsmen who made use of the smaller file. Orders from William Barrow show that as early as 1779 Stubs was meeting the demands of dentists, and in 1798 a customer at Hull asked for " files for taking the decayed part out of teeth by twisting them round ".

Common files, such as were required by blacksmiths, were not produced by Stubs. But large files were sometimes sent to the order of stone-masons ; and a considerable trade was done in those for the use of shoemakers at Kendal, Manchester and Rochdale. The rising iron and steel industry also provided a valuable market : in 1795, Mark Gilpin, manager of the Coalbrookdale Ironworks, sent the first of a long series of orders ; and in the following year the Carron Iron Company wrote to say that they had been recommended to Stubs as a maker of excellent files, that they wished to have 100 dozen immediately, and that larger orders should follow.

---

[1] " The bounty of nature on Sheffield town smiles,
Yet could other trades work if we did not make files ? "
asked a Sheffield rhymester, Alexander Stephens, about 1780. See *The Songs of Joseph Mather*, 91 n.

Far more important, however, than any demand yet mentioned was that which came from workers in wood. Pit-saw, frame-saw, and whip-saw files were supplied to the Ashton factors in 1778; and in later years orders came from all parts of the country. In 1793 William Naylor Wright, a celebrated ship-builder of Liverpool, became a customer; in 1795 Thomas Kirkup of Sunderland asked to have an order executed immediately " as we are building barricks for soldiers all of wood "; and in the same year a Thomas Stobbart wrote for supplies for the Duke of Bridgewater, whose sawyers, Stubs was told, gave the *P.S.* file " preference over all others ". With the sawyers, as with others, there was a strong tendency to cut out the middleman and buy direct.[1] Moreover, in a trade in which the tradition of the journeyman gild was still strong, it is not surprising that men who had to provide their own tools sometimes made use of their craft organization to supply their needs co-operatively. The following letter (addressed " Mr. P. Stobs, Patent File Maker, Liverpool.") illustrates the tendency.

EDENBURGH 24*th Aprail* 1796.

SIR,

As we the Sawers in Eden[r] have joined our selves into an Incorporated body we therefore mean you this accoumpt to furnish our selves in our own tools and we therefore have agreed to give you the first offer as to furnisheng us with fiells and we flatter our selves that you you [sic] will serve us as well and as reasonable as posably you can, and as we have dealt in your fiels for this Good many years we still mean to continue if so be you do serve us well and as there his bean great compleants on them for this some years past ever sence they came to the redused price we are Resolved t'ether to pay the former price and have them as good as before. But as we are at a loss to fiend a proper Derections for you we wish you to writ us and let us know to derect you and which way the money is to be trancemitted to you as we mean to pay the (   ) immediately on receiving the goods likewise you (   ) what is the price of the Gross of them as we mean to take only one Gross for the first time.

So we expect to hear from you soon and let us know the way best to be done with regeard of receiving the goods and paying the Money and you may depend on receiving your Money by derecting your letters to John M[c] Intosh, Sawer, head of the Cannongate Eden[r] where the goods will be taken in and the Money paid by your Derection.

No more at Praisent
But remains your Most Hum. and obed[t] Serv[t]

JOHN M[c] INTOSH, Deacon
J. PITTENDRIGH, Clk.

---

[1] " There is but few files wanted now as sawyers and others is all getting themselves from England ", wrote Archibald Turner of Glasgow in 1799.

Further evidence of the corporate activities of the sawyers is provided by a letter of 28 February, 1799, from William Betteney, Clerk to the Friendly United Society of Sawyers of Stockport, containing an order for 12 dozen files which were to be sent to the *Unicorn Inn* in Lower Hillgate.

Among the largest consumers of Warrington files were the men who were busy transforming the technique of the cotton industry on the basis of the factory system. Sometimes the files were for the use of the millwrights, joiners and others who were erecting the factories; but there was also a continuous demand for use in the mills themselves, since every spindle had to be filed to ensure easy running in the bolster. In 1790 Samuel Greg sent an order from the cotton mill he had set up, three years earlier, at Styal; in 1791 Peter Drinkwater's Piccadilly Factory in Manchester, the Salford Engine Twist Co., and the mill of Peel, Wilks & Co. at Tamworth were all furnished with *P.S.* files; in 1792 an engineer, G. Newbold, sent an order on behalf of the Rawlight Mill Co.; in 1793 David Dale bought files for the New Lanark Mills; in 1794 the Mold Cotton Twist Co. became a customer; and in 1797 the firm of Peel Yates & Co. of Burrs Mill, Radcliffe,[1] was added to the list.

Besides the orders sent by manufacturers direct many others came from local dealers who supplied the mills in their own neighbourhood. The machine-makers of Glasgow were also good customers of Stubs, and in 1792 Daniel Mackay, described as spindle- and fly-maker of Garret Lane, Manchester, asked for supplies suitable for filing steel spindles in lathes.[2] The boom in the erection of spinning factories in the early seventeen-nineties must, indeed, have been one of the most important extraneous factors in the building up of the fortunes of Peter Stubs.

Apart from files, tools of all kinds were supplied to ironmongers and dealers in many parts of the country. Where, as in the case of awls for the use of shoemakers, the demand was substantial, it paid Stubs to employ outworkers and so draw a manufacturer's as well as a

[1] Modern writers usually speak of this as the Bury Mill. But in 1797 the manager of the firm complained that a letter from Stubs had been delayed 21 days owing to mis-direction. He asked that future letters should be addressed " Radcliffe, nr. Manchester ", and that no mention should be made of Bury " as we have a post at Radcliffe ".

[2] Even in areas untouched by the new technique, where yarn was still spun by domestic workers, there was a demand for files : in 1794 a Samuel Gaskell ordered a small number for Samuel Barrett of Woore (Staffordshire) explaining that " he puts out sping. for us and when there is any money due to him will pay you for them ".

trader's profit. But, generally, he acted as an agent, buying tools from independent producers, and selling at a price 5 or 10 per cent. higher than that at which he bought.[1] At one time or another he supplied knives for shoemakers at Kendal ; pliers for stocking-makers at Leicester ; nippers for fustian-cutters at Manchester ; " dumbies " for silk-workers at Congleton ; gauges for pin-makers at Blackburn ; and callipers, dividers and hand-vices for craftsmen in various towns. Particularly large dealings were done in the appliances and materials of watch- and clock-makers' arbors, pinions, broaches and so on. The boom in mill-construction brought a demand for cotton spindles from Glasgow in 1792 and from Paisley in 1795. In the following year James Sword of Glasgow announced that he meant to do a big business in spindles and asked Stubs to recommend a maker with whom he could deal direct [2] ; and, again, in the period of rapid building of factories in 1802 there was an active demand for spindles. In 1798 Warham, Potts & Co. of Leeds ordered pulleys for use in their hair-seating manufactory [3] ; and orders for wire from various dealers were so extensive that, after 1802, when the workshops in Warrington were set up, Stubs found it profitable to add wire-drawing to his own industrial activities.

At an early period Peter Stubs discovered that the connection he had built up with ironmongers and others could serve as a means of disposing of goods of various kinds sent to him by business friends. In 1791, for example, a quantity of glue was sold for James Sword of Glasgow, and in 1798 a consignment of hats was put up to auction for B. Meanley of Rochdale. More important was a regular trade in horn and ivory combs which was established by Stubs in 1805 : the combs were bought at a discount of $7\frac{1}{2}$ or 10 per cent. from two concerns, Butler & Bate and Banner & Doke of St. Helens, and were sold to retailers in various parts of the country. About the same time the growing demand for popular education and the rise of the Sunday School movement opened up a new channel of profitable trade. On

---

[1] In February, 1805, Z. Rowton of Northampton wrote : " When you chd. me a Commission upon Hands and Verges in last did you not forget the Disct. you receive *off* them ? I cannot have any objection to pay 5 p. cent Commission when *that is deducted.*"

[2] Tenders were obtained by Stubs from Robert Farrand of Oldham, who asked 26s. a gross for 11-inch spindles, and from William Row-bottom of the same place, who was willing to supply them at 22s. a gross.

[3] They asked that the holes should be bored exactly in the middle and added that they were dissatisfied with pulleys they had previously had from Liverpool because the holes were bored to one side.

13 April, 1805, a letter was received from Wright & Hazelhurst of Runcorn in which they said, " Understanding you employ a person in the capacity of Traveller, we being Manufacturers of Writing Slates could wish to form a kind of connection for that article and it might be done at the same time as he is doing your business as we suppose is business is chiefly with Ironmongers and they being the principal dealers of this article. If this proposal meets your approbation, we will one of us come over, and fix at what rate of commission we could allow, we send^g the goods of according to is orders."

Terms satisfactory to both parties were quickly arranged, and letters from Joseph Wood, the traveller for Stubs, show that slates and slate pencils were being sold to customers in such towns as Stockport, Ashton-under-Lyne, Huddersfield, Dewsbury, Lincoln, Leicester, Belfast and Perth. At first the arrangement was that Stubs should receive a commission of 10 per cent. ; but it was soon found better to buy the goods outright, leaving, however, the work of packing and delivery to the manufacturers. Wright & Hazelhurst undertook not to have any direct dealings with customers obtained by Stubs, and when, in April, 1806, Cort & Barston of Leicester wrote them for a price-list they replied that they were under such a contract with Stubs and referred the would-be clients to him.

At one time or another Stubs is to be seen selling to particular customers other commodities, ranging from a cast-iron bookcase and glass cylinders for an electrical machine to potatoes and cokernuts. It might, indeed, have appeared that the story of his business, like that of many others at this period, was to be one of evolution from specialized manufacture to general merchanting. The reputation which he had built up as a craftsman was, however, too great to be lightly relinquished ; and both he and his successors were careful to see that, whatever other activities they might engage in, these must remain subordinate to the prime concern of manufacturing files of the first quality.

III

Peter Stubs had to sell his files in competition with the manufacturers of Liverpool and, to some extent, with those of Sheffield. The number of merchant file-makers in Lancashire was, however, sufficiently small for it to be possible to limit the sphere of rivalry, and by 1792 there is evidence that meetings were being held to regulate prices. On 10 October of that year, Carolus Charles, writing of the Liverpool file-makers, said, " They all beg you'll agree with them in advancing the price of files and desires you'll let me know in your next and I'll communicate it to them. They say Messrs. Green, Tarleton, Mather and

Webster are all agreeable to do it.   If you'll joine with them it will be done very quickly." [1]   A few days later, on 27 October, Charles expressed the opinion that the other manufacturers were too sanguine in their expectations and added, " I dare say Sheffield people wou'd be upon us if we rais'd 'em."   But Stubs was evidently willing to run the risk, for letters received from customers a few weeks afterwards make reference to the advance that had taken place.

It is probable that the prices of Lancashire files were regulated by concerted action of the manufacturers throughout the whole of the following decade.   Like others, Stubs sent out printed price-lists, and in October, 1800, a London customer, John Morley, of Covent Garden, mentioned that the prices in one of these which had been sent him were the same as those of other houses he had done business with in Liverpool and Prescot : he added that he depended on Stubs' allowing him the same discount of 15 per cent.

In 1801 Stubs himself appears to have taken the initiative in calling a meeting of the Lancashire file-manufacturers.   On 7 March, 1801, Messrs. Mather & Lasselles of Liverpool replied to a letter from him as follows :

Your favour we duly receiv'd this Day, and we have not had an opportunity to see the rest of our Brethren in the trade, but will do it as soon as possible and will communicate to you the result in consequence thereof as to time and place of meeting together, and we are very much oblig'd to you for your kindness in the Affair, as we have had some thoughts some time back that *files* ought and *must* be advanc'd.

A few days later William Gant, of Messrs. Lancaster & Gant of Prescot, replied to an invitation to the conference in words which support the belief that there was some permanent form of organization among the file-makers and tool-manufacturers of west Lancashire, and perhaps that this was organized in branches according to particular products :

If you think my attendance of any serves I shall attend at any place and time appointed.   As the branch of filemaking dose not belong to me, I can't be so proper a judge in the price as those brought up in it.

---

[1] Tarleton was celebrated as a watch-maker.   " The late Mr. William Tarleton was the first person who brought the manufacture of Liverpool watches into high repute ; since which period, several extensive concerns for the manufacture and sale of watches and chronometers have been established, and are carried on with success."—Henry Smithers : *Liverpool, its Commerce, Statistics and Institutions* (1825), 189.

You, Lassel, Molyneux and the Remainder of the Branch will be most proper.[1]

The file-makers of Sheffield held meetings of their own. Stubs was not directly interested in the prices of the larger files made of common steel; but some of the Sheffield manufacturers who made small files of cast steel were in direct competition with him, and it was, therefore, important that he should know what they were about. From time to time customers in Sheffield sent him information. Thus, on 23 May, 1796, James Cam wrote, " At a general meeting of the Master File Manufacturers it was unanimously agreed that in consequence of the very high price of iron and other articles used in the manufacturing of Files that [sic] an advance was quite necessary." He enclosed a list of the prices agreed upon at the meeting. Again, in February, 1799, a Joseph Pashley sent Stubs the prices of manufacture and sale in Sheffield with the comment that he had been " ill put about to get them ". A year later, in February, 1800, John Harrison & Son mentioned that the Sheffield makers had increased the prices of files and recommended Stubs to follow suit. And, on 27 May, 1803, a Sheffield customer (and competitor) Daniel Doncaster wrote, " Perhaps you have been informed of the advance in steel which is 6 pounds p. ton higher, in consequence whereof we have advanced files to the prices of 1801, say 12 In. 9/6 and 14 In. 14/– and so on in proportion ".[2] Stubs was quite aware of it, for, according to a printed tariff, the Lancashire file-makers had already held a " Public Meeting " on 9 May and had agreed on the higher prices that were to come into effect on 1 June.

Other lists, printed in Prescot, show that the prices of watch-makers' tools were similarly regulated. One of these, dated 20 January, 1800, relates to a wide variety of instruments, gauges and so on; another of 1 September, 1802, gives the prices of dividers and screw-plates; and yet another of 1 December, 1802, those of watch-makers' and clock-makers' broaches. There is evidence, moreover, that just as the Lancashire file-makers kept their eyes on Sheffield and adjusted their prices in conformity with those fixed there, so the makers of small tools in the Midlands tried to maintain contact with Lancashire. In January, 1803, W. Whitmore & Son of Birmingham enquired " if the prices of different articles are fully established in your

[1] William Molyneux was the celebrated watch-file maker of Rainhill.
[2] Before the advance 12-inch files had been selling at 8s. 6d. and 14-inch at 13s. a dozen.

Country " and asked to be supplied with a list, " or, if you cannot furnish us with a General List, send such as are in circulation, with your opinion of the propriety of the advance of Tools, for our direction, as we would not be the first to advance, nor would we by any means undersell ".

Regulation of prices by concerted action did not, of course, preclude rivalry in sales. So long as competition was fair Stubs had little to fear, for the superiority of his product was acknowledged. " I have other makers' files, but I must do you Justice—none so much preferr'd ", wrote William Cooke of Burnley in 1794 ; and it would not be difficult to find many testimonials of a similar tenor in the letters of other satisfied customers. Quite early in the career of Peter Stubs, however, some of his rivals, and those of Sheffield in particular, were guilty of a practice from which Sheffield itself has suffered perhaps more than any other manufacturing centre in the world. In March, 1791, a Huddersfield customer, John Booth, informed Stubs that the local sawyers were getting from Bradford files of other makers on which the initials *P.S.* had been stamped. A year later a firm of ironmongers at Greenock remarked that they had had files from a Sheffield house marked *P.S.* but that Mr. Warham (of Warham, Potts & Co. of Leeds) had said that the genuine files of Stubs " would be superior to them as silver to copper ". In 1793 Thomas Morris of Ruabon wrote to the same effect : files with the letters *P.S.*, somewhat larger than the initials on Stubs' own dies, were on sale at Wrexham. In 1794 Thomas Kirkup of Sunderland reported that " Sheffield firms stamp P.S. mark " and mentioned a business house the name of which (since it still survives and is highly respected in Sheffield to-day) will not be disclosed here. As time went on this practice of false marking increased. In May, 1799, William Horsfall of Barnsley told Stubs that " your mark is immitated by numbers of file makers " ; and in February, 1800, an old friend John Harrison of Sheffield wrote, " We find it's very common with many of our makers to stamp them P.S. and they have often want'd us to have them mark'd so, but can safely say we never sent any such away to our knowledge, tho' I find our Factors commonly impose on their friends in this manner."

The evil was a difficult one to combat ; and perhaps Peter Stubs was of too easy-going a nature to trouble much about it. But in 1805, when he was nearing his end, control of the business came to be exer- cised by a man of determination. " Your son John ", wrote an old customer and friend [1] this year, " would draw blood from flint." It was almost certainly on the initiative of John Stubs that measures

[1] John Whitley, of Clowes & Whitley.

were at last taken to deal with the Sheffield counterfeiters. On 8 October a warning that the menace was increasing had come from Shaw & Marshall : " So many files are made in this neighbourhood marked P.S. that your trade must suffer considerably, and you should take some steps to remedy this growing evil or your files will get out of repute in the end." A fortnight later, on 24 October, the following notice appeared in the columns of the *Iris or the Sheffield Advertiser*. It was repeated in the two succeeding weekly issues.

A CAUTION
TO FILE MANUFACTURERS

Whereas several in this trade in the Town and Neighbourhood of Sheffield have made it their practice, for some time past, to stamp on their Files the Initials of my name, and have afterwards imposed upon Shopkeepers and others, by selling them as Files of my Manufacture, calling them Lancashire Files ; in consequence of which I am receiving injury daily ; I therefore take this method of informing the trade in general, and those of Sheffield and its neighbourhood in particular, who have been guilty of this practice, that I feel justly indignant at such conduct, and that I mean to use every endeavour to detect such unlawful practices in future, and, whenever I do, I intend to commence an action or actions (*as I am by Counsel already advised*) against any person or persons who shall be guilty of such dishonourable subterfuges in future.

WARRINGTON, *October* 10, 1805.   PETER STUBS.

A mere warning, however, was not sufficient. On 2 November, Eyre, Hall & Smith wrote from Sheffield saying, " Notwithstanding your advertisement in the newspaper applications are still made to manufacturers of Files here to mark your initials ", and they urged the need to offer a considerable award for information if the offenders were to be brought to justice. Possibly the illness and death of Stubs were responsible for the delay in giving effect to this advice. But on 3 April, 1806, another notice was inserted in the *Iris*, which read :

FIFTY POUNDS
REWARD

Several File Manufacturers, in Sheffield and other Places, have, for some time past, been in the habit of marking their files P.S. and imposing them upon the Public, as Files made by Peter Stubs.

The above Reward will be given to any person giving such information as shall lead to a conviction of the offender or offenders, by application to John Stubs, for the Executors of the late Peter Stubs.

WARRINGTON, *March* 26, 1806.

Whether or not this offer achieved its object the records do not disclose. The infringement of trade marks is a perennial evil, and makers besides Stubs suffered from it not only individually but collectively, for tools made in other parts of the country sometimes bore the imprint " Lancashire ". It was perhaps one of the functions of the embryo association of file and tool manufacturers to combat piracy of this kind, or, possibly, a separate organization was set up, similar to the Society for the Preservation of Marks which had been established in Sheffield in 1791.[1] No direct evidence of corporate action in such matters has, indeed, been discovered ; but a reference to seals used as a guarantee of origin appears in a letter of 29 March, 1805, in which Thomas Barlow & Co. of Manchester inform Stubs that " each packet is to have the Seal of genuine Liverpool files "—" Liverpool " in this connection obviously embracing Warrington.

A minor trouble of a similar nature arose from the desire of some customers to have their own initials or marks stamped on the wares, instead of those of the manufacturer. " If you ever stamp T on your files it would please prejudiced people ", wrote James Dowell of Bristol in March, 1793—the " T " probably being the mark of Samuel Timmins of Birmingham, through whom Dowell had previously obtained his files.[2] In April, 1796, Walker & Beck of London instructed Stubs to mark the files they ordered *W & B only* and complained that a previous consignment had been stamped *P.S.* ; and, once more, in November, 1798, Dowell asked Stubs to stamp files supplied to him *JD* " and take this request as a compliment ". Whether Stubs was flattered or not we have no means of knowing. But, since he was himself in competition with the merchants who sold his files, he can hardly have looked with favour on such attempts to capture his good-will. Dowell and Walker & Beck had large foreign connections and the name of Peter Stubs was not yet well known abroad. But the high reputation which had been won by the initials *P.S.* in Britain makes it probable that most dealers in the home market would prefer that files supplied to them should bear the stamp of their origin. The problem of customers' marks was never, therefore, a serious one for Peter Stubs.

[1] G. I. H. Lloyd : *The Cutlery Trades*, 144.
[2] Mathias Spencer of Sheffield marked his files *T*, and it is possible that it was his files that Stubs was asked to counterfeit.

CHAPTER SIX

THE INN

THE date at which Peter Stubs became an innkeeper is not known. All that the records disclose is that at least as early as 1788 he was occupying the *White Bear* in Bridge Street, which he leased from Thomas Watt, chandler and soap-boiler of Warrington. The amount paid for the tenancy at this time is uncertain.[1] But a few years later, between 1794 and 1801, the annual rent was 50 guineas, payable in two unequal instalments : 22½ guineas in May and 27½ guineas in November. The inn must have been a very busy place, for, like most other publicans of his day, Stubs was much more than a mere vendor of liquors. He bought barley and hops, made his own malt, brewed his own ale and beer, and sold barley, hops, malt and yeast on a fairly considerable scale. And in spite of his absorption with the details of file-making, he found time, it would appear, to share in the social and convivial activities that are part of the tradition of the English inn.

Just as in his file business Stubs drew his raw materials from many different sources, so in his business as maltster and brewer. During the season beginning in October, 1794, for example, he bought barley from no fewer than 25 different persons. Some of these, it is clear, were farmers or landowners in the immediate vicinity of Warrington, and with these business dealings were carried on without the help of any intermediary factor or merchant. But other suppliers were more remote ; and, in his later years, at least, Stubs found it worth while to employ agents who visited growers in Cheshire, made purchases, and saw to such matters as sacking and transport. In the year 1800 his friend William Cole was collecting supplies of barley for him at Chester ; about the same time Jonathan Hockenhull was buying for him in the markets at Nantwich and Whitchurch ; and between February and April 1803, John Betley visited farmers about the River Weaver and carried barley (to the value of £339) in carts to Warrington.

---

[1] A bill for six months' rent, dated 1 August, 1789, is for £21 7s. 6d. It would not be safe, however, to assume that the annual rent was double this sum.

More important, however, were the supplies obtained through a number of merchants in Liverpool who imported barley from the eastern and southern counties, from Scotland, Ireland and the Baltic, and sent it in flats along the Mersey Navigation. By dealing with them Stubs was saved much incidental trouble and was, moreover, able to obtain varieties of grain, each specially suited to the making of a particular product. Of his aggregate purchases, valued at over £1,300, in the season 1794–5, more than three-quarters came from five such merchants : the bill for William Carter alone was £299 1s. 11d. and that for Corrie, Gladstone & Bradshaw £290 9s. 4d.[1]

From an early period Stubs sought to push past the Liverpool merchants to dealers situated nearer to the main sources of supply. Here his connections in the file trade were of help. Already in 1789 he had established relations with a J. Newton of Newark, who bought files of him and who kept him informed of the prices of barley as quoted each week in the *Stamford Mercury* ; and in 1795 his friends Eyre, Hall & Smith of Sheffield sent him advice as to the Mansfield market. In 1789 he was buying barley direct of James Gothard of Stone, and by 1793 he had established an account with Joseph Barber of Walsall. Two years later he made purchases to the value of nearly £500 of A. P. Sharp of Rugeley ; in 1797 he had dealings with Joseph Orton of Polesworth, near Tamworth ; and in 1798 George Webb of Hill Ridware, near Lichfield, was given large orders. In the east of England the more important of those with whom he dealt in the 'nineties were John Blundell of Lincoln, and Caparn, Barber & Hare of Newark. And when, in 1799–1801, crop failures led to difficulties in obtaining adequate supplies from these sources, he bought from other firms in various parts of the country.[2]

In some cases the dealers bought outright and sold to Stubs at a profit ; in others they bought on his account and were remunerated

---

[1] William Carter is described in the Liverpool Directories of the period as a corn merchant of Dale Street, and Corrie, Gladstone & Bradshaw appear as corn factors of George's Dock Gates. John Gladstone, who had joined Edgar Corrie in the corn trade in 1786, was the father of William Ewart Gladstone. Among other Liverpool merchants or factors with whom Stubs had dealings, at one time or another, were Thomas Alison & Co., Backhouse & Robinson, Bold, Richard & Conway, Thomas Booth & Co., Hannay & Logan, Hodgson & Pearson, Lickbarrow & Wright, Thompson & Affleck and Wright & Davies.

[2] From Henry Gardiner of Norwich, Thomas Hodson of Newark, A. & J. Bowker of Lynn, John Edwards of Worcester, Aris & Taylor of Oxford, John Robinson of Ulverston and George Lowther & Son of Dornock, Dumfries.

by a commission. Most of them were willing to adopt either method. In November, 1797, for example, Joseph Orton of Polesworth offered to sell to Stubs at a price not less than 8*s*. a measure (of 36 quarts) or to buy on commission—" lett it be which you please I will do the best layeth in my powers for you ". The commission actually charged by George Webb of Hill Ridware in 1799 was 1*d*. a measure, which, since the price at which he bought was 4*s*. 1½*d*., worked out at about 2 per cent. ; and in the same year George Lowther & Son of Dornock asked 1*d*. per Winchester bushel, or 3*d*. per Carlisle bushel, as payment for their trouble in purchasing and shipping. The advantages of dealing in this way were set forth by Henry Gardiner in a printed circular in 1800 :

My plan of business being, to purchase on the lowest terms I can, per Commission, of the Growers, and small Dealers, I am persuaded you will invariably find it more to your interest, to have Corn purchased in this way, than to request offers ; indeed there is a very essential difference in the nature of the business—it is obviously my interest to quote the lowest currency, at which I could purchase ; whilst in making offers, the exact reverse is invariably presented to you ; by fixing the very highest price at which you may happen to be thought likely to purchase.

Whichever method was adopted, speedy payment—speedy compared with practice in the file trade—was expected. The Liverpool merchants, as well as those in the other centres, usually stipulated for a bill at two months' on delivery of the grain, though on one occasion in 1795 Robert Gladstone allowed Stubs to deduct two months' interest from a bill payable two months ahead. Where barley was bought on commission the terms of credit were sometimes even shorter : in 1799 George Lowther & Sons asked for " good bills at 1 month date " with which to pay the farmers from whom they had bought.

Weights and measures varied so greatly between markets, and one consignment of barley might differ so much in quality from another, that it would be profitless to attempt to trace the course of prices over the years. Attention may, however, be drawn to two special features affecting the market. The first is the extent to which price was dependent on supplies actually brought to market. In October of each year, when (as was pointed out to Stubs by correspondents as far apart in time as 1789 and 1800) farmers were too busy threshing and sowing wheat to come to town, there was a tendency for prices to rise, and this tendency was, no doubt, strengthened by the fact that, since the malting season began in October, the shortage of supply happened to coincide with an intense demand. The second feature was the dependence of the price of barley on that of other grain. For barley was a food-crop as well as a drink-crop, and in years when there was a deficiency of wheat the price of barley also soared. Such was the case in 1799–1801. Wet summers and the embargo on Russian grain led to extreme shortage ; and the demand for barley by the millers was such that the supplies available for malting were severely contracted. In December, 1798, Stubs bought barley of Mrs. Heron of Daresbury, at 5s. a measure ; in January, 1800, he paid her 8s. a measure, and prices subsequently went much higher. In October, 1800, George Webb of Hill Ridware reported that there were " several buyers for one seller " ; the farmers were now " quite Masters " ; they refused to supply sacks as had been the custom, and if Stubs wanted barley he must send his own bags. A week or two later John Robinson of Ulverston declined an order, saying that the farmers expected to sell their barley for food at a high price, as they had done the previous year ; in November, John Edwards of Worcester reported that most of the local barley was being ground for bread, and George Webb referred to purchases by " subscriptions " for the sale of meal to the poor below cost. By January, 1801, Stubs was paying as much as 13s. 6d. a bushel for grain he could have had at 5s. a few years earlier.

In such circumstances, malting was brought to a standstill in many districts. Even if a dealer were able to obtain malting barley it might be unwise to attempt to move it to the kilns. For food riots were widespread. " I think at present it wd. be atended with some little danger in sending it," wrote Jonathan Hockenhull from Nantwich " the lower Order of People seem so dissatisfied." The shortage was intensified locally (as Peter Stubs junior informed his father in a letter from Liverpool in February, 1801) by the difficulty in getting sailors to man the ships : " they cannot persuade the Seamen to come here, the Impress being so very warm ". Although prices fell considerably in the Spring of 1801, it was not until after the signing of the Peace in October that they reached what was considered the normal level again.

As far as one can see, Peter Stubs weathered the crisis without great hardship. He was a valued customer of the dealers, and when these were no longer able to obtain barley for him some of them allowed him to purchase malt—at high prices, it is true—from their own dwindling stocks. He can hardly, however, have been happy, for he was not usually a buyer of malt, and the high reputation which his ale had acquired would seem to have depended largely on the skill with which he turned the barley into malt at his own kilns in Warrington.

The markets in which Stubs bought his hops were similarly scattered.

From time to time dealers from the western and west-Midland counties visited Warrington with samples and obtained orders. In 1789 Stubs made purchases of John Corbett of Greve, near Bromyard in Herefordshire, and from 1790 onward he was a regular customer of Oakes & Bangham of Bridgnorth, Edward Dixon of Dudley, John Edwards of Lindridge and Stephen Barber of Walsall. In May, 1798, John Eyre (of Eyre, Hall & Smith of Sheffield) wrote recommending a new source of supply: " Would not good North Clay Hops meet with ready sale in your part of the World. Mrs. Eyre's Brother lives in what is called the North Clays near Retford and grows some himself and in general of a good quality and the price he is now selling for is 6 Guineas p. Cwt.—if you think any good could be done, should have no objection to join in a Speculation next Retford Hop Fair, as he is a person who has a thorough knowledge of that Trade and would give us every assistance in his power." Whether or not such a speculation took place is uncertain ; but shortly afterwards a letter from the grain factors, Caparn, Barber & Hare shows that Stubs was buying North Clay hops in Newark.

As with barley, so with hops, the terms of credit were short : payment had usually to be made by a bill at two months' immediately on delivery of the cargo. The merchants bought on their own account of the planters and sold to Stubs at a profit : there is no evidence of purchases on commission. The times of brisk buying naturally coincided with those for the buying of barley : the season opened in October after the crop had been harvested and at a time when brewers, no doubt, were beginning to think of the Christmas trade. If the conditions of 1794 were normal it would appear that the growers disposed of about half their stock in October, holding back the remainder so as to be able to profit by any rise in demand which might occur later in the season. In a letter of 28 October Humphrey Oakes said that 40,000 pockets, or about half the total crop of Worcester hops, had already been sold. " The planters ", he added, " will speculate on a Quarter, so that we have but another Quarter to supply the Mark^t with for 6 months to come."

The price of hops naturally depended on the state of the crops, and in years when there was a shortage of barley and hops the price of both was high. A sudden rise in the price of one would, however, tend to depress that of the other. " In consequence of the unexpected high prices of grain, hops have long been much reduced in price ", wrote Stephen Barber of Walsall in February, 1800 ; and in December of the same year John Edwards of Worcester expressed the same thing by saying " as Barley is so high and their stock is verry small hops are lower on account of Malt being so dear and scarce ". That the prices of two commodities in joint demand should tend to vary in inverse ratio with each other is a truism to the modern economist ; but it is not without interest to find the principle enunciated by practical men at the end of the eighteenth century.

Of the barley which Stubs purchased a small part was sold, unchanged in form, to James Robinson, a local maltster, to John Atherton, who supplied Stubs with coal and charcoal, and to smaller customers who, no doubt, made their own arrangements for malting. Among the last of these were several of the file-cutters and forgers employed by Stubs : an entry in the *Malt Book* dated 15 February, 1796, relates to the sale of 8½ measures (at 7s. a measure) to the " Shop men ", and another of the following day to that of 5 measures to Cranage, Cook, Sutton and Griffith. Were such workmen, one wonders, able to turn the barley into malt in their own homes, or was the reason for their buying crude barley that they had discovered some other way of evading the high duties imposed on the professional maltster ?

By far the larger part of his barley was, however, converted into malt by Stubs himself. From an early period he had rented two kilns : one in Sankey Street, for which he paid, in 1790 and subsequent years, a rent of £6 a year to the executors of Miss Dolly Patten [1] ; the other in the Buttermarket for which, from 1793, he paid a rent of £10 to John Boyer. Other kiln-rents were paid to John Dumbell of the Mersey Mills in 1793 and to a John Clayton in 1797. A letter from George Webb of Hill Ridware shows that, in August, 1799, Stubs was seeking expert advice as to the erection of a new kiln, and that he was also trying to find a west-country maltster to come and work for him in Warrington.[2] From time to time the services of other local maltsters were employed, as in 1794, when Peter Chrimes turned 100 payable measures of barley into malt at 3½d. a measure and James Robinson did the same at a price of 4d. a measure.

The process of malting consisted of steeping the barley in water to make it germinate and then drying it in the kiln—at a low temperature if it was required for pale liquors, at a higher one if it was for

---

[1] A member of the Patten family of Bank Hall, whose house is now the Town Hall of Warrington.

[2] Webb reported that he had inquired at several places for a good maltster and that the only one he had found was a master who was reduced in circumstances because " he loves ale and does not know when he has had enough ". In a letter of December, however, Webb mentioned that he had heard of a workman who, he thought, would answer the purpose : he was " just com'n off from the Suplementary Militia, a drawn man ".

dark ones. It was important that the malt should not be contaminated by fumes, and the fuel used at the kiln was therefore charcoal and not coal.[1]

After it had been taken from the kiln the malt was sent to the miller to be ground into a coarse meal. One Thomas Langshaw was generally employed in this process and Stubs paid him at the rate of 1d. a bushel. Then the malt was carried to the *White Bear*, where it was put into " mash " or " maslin " pans and mixed with warm water. The resultant wort was pumped into leaden vats, hops were added, and the whole was boiled. Next, the liquor was passed through a cooler, barm was introduced to effect fermentation, and, after the scum had been removed, the ale was run into barrels ready to send to customers at a distance or to be tapped and sold by retail at the bar of the inn.[2] Brewing took place every third or fourth day throughout the year and 22 or 30 measures of malt were used each time. In the early days, at least, it was performed by Edward Unsworth, who had also other duties to perform at the inn : a memorandum in a *File Workmen's Book* records that " Edward is to do the necessary Brewing and to keep the yard &c. clean and is to have 10/6 p week House rent and Fire for 11 Months from the 15th Sep. 1791 and to Hostle and to have the ostling money ".

Malting was subject to heavy taxation. Stubs had to pay £3 a year for the licences on two kilns and a duty of 1s. 4¼d. per Winchester bushel of malt produced. In addition there were heavy duties on brewing, amounting to 8s. a barrel for ale, 3s. a barrel for table beer, and 1s. 4d. a gallon for small beer. Private individuals, brewing for their own use and not for sale, were, however, exempt from the beer (though not, of course, from the malt) duty ; and hence most of those who could afford the necessary equipment bought malt and hops, brewed at home, and thus avoided about half the total duty imposed on the whole process of turning barley into beer. The result was that the main incidence of the taxes fell on the poorer classes who had to buy their beer from publicans.[3]

This feature of the system of taxation explains why so large a part of the business conducted by Stubs at the *White Bear* consisted of the sale of malt. It is not possible to give any statement of the quantity of ale and beer sold by him ; but the following figures—the result

---

[1] It was supplied by John Atherton as well as by a Widow Jameson.

[2] In 1796 a local plumber, Robert White, provided 3 cwts. 1 qr. 10 lb. of lead for the brew pan (at 2¾d. a pound), 8½ lb. of solder for the mash tub, and 3½ lb. of solder for the pipes of the cooler.

[3] *McCulloch's Commercial Dictionary s.v.* Ale and Malt.

of many tedious additions of individual purchases, sales and payments recorded in the *Malt Book*—suggest that malting played a considerably larger part than brewing in his economy.[1]

	1794–5	1795–6	1796–7
Barley bought			
Measures	—	5,169½	4,871¾
Value	£1,321 6s. 5½d.	£1,553 7s. 9½d.	£1,154 12s. 1½d.
Barley sold			
Measures	282	217	42½
Value	£71 7s. 2½d.	£67 6s. 5d.	£9 14s. 9d.
Malt sold			
Measures	3,347	3,449⅝	3,282¼
Value [2]	£1,204 1s. 2½d.	£1,323 6s. 0d.	£1,087 2s. 10½d.
Malt brewed			
Measures	1,745	2,196	1,994¾
Malting Duty	£337 7s. 4½d.	£367 5s. 2¾d.	£342 3s. 4½d.

Many tributes were paid to the quality of the malt produced by Stubs. In 1799, for instance, the Rev. H. Kirkpatrick of Park Lane wrote, " I prefer your Malt to any other persons' ", and in 1802 F. W. Mallalieu of Manchester wrote, " I assure you so great is our confidence in your knowledge of this article that we can think well of none else." Most customers ordered hops along with the malt—usually a pound of hops to each measure of malt. The market was extensive : an Account Book for the years 1792–7 contains more than 130, and another for 1797–1802 more than 260, names of individual customers. Prominent among these were several retailers of ale and beer in Warrington and neighbouring towns.[3] Landed families, like the Herons of Daresbury Hall and the Pattens of Bank Hall also obtained their supplies from Stubs : Mrs. Heron's purchases came to more than £100 a year, a sum which surely meant that she was brewing not only for personal consumption but also for that of the servants on the estate. And the same was true of Rev. H. Kirkpatrick who, in

[1] The accounts for the sale of barley are for the season beginning in April of each year ; those for the purchase of barley, the sale and brewing of malt and the malting duty are for the season beginning in October.

[2] Including the value of hops sold. This was of small consequence : in 1794–5, Stubs sold 656¼ lbs. of hops, which at 1s. per lb. yielded him £32 16s. 3d.

[3] Among them John Harrison of the *Rose and Crown* and Joseph Garner of the *Blue Bell*, Warrington ; John Brown of the *Nag's Head* in Jackson's Row, Henry Harrison of the *Red Lion* in Deansgate, John Harrop of the *Blue Bell* in High Street, Manchester ; and Michael Hunt of the *Legs of Man* in Gravel Lane, Salford.

August, 1798, sent an urgent request for malt and hops, saying
" My mowers and haymakers have almost drank me dry." [1]

Whether to save themselves trouble, or because his product was
better than any they could themselves brew, some innkeepers and
other middle-class customers bought ales and beer of Stubs. Thus
John Harrop of Manchester sometimes wrote for some of Stubs'
" excellent October " to sell at his own inn ; William Harris of Ashton
ordered supplies of what he called Stubs' " nappy brown Ale " ; and
in 1798 a Macclesfield wholesale dealer in liquors inquired whether
Stubs ever sent any of his best ale to other than private houses and,
if so, at what price he was willing to supply it. Stubs' ale, like his
malt, was evidently highly approved. " We are so used to your brew
that I am afraid no other will please ", wrote William Pownall of
Liverpool in 1796, " I should take £20 p. annum from you. It has
already saved many dozens of wine in course of year."

At the present day the distinction between ale and beer is difficult
to draw. Experts who have been consulted—and experts in this
field are many—differ among themselves ; and some declare that ale
and beer are one and the same thing. But in the days of Peter Stubs
there must have been a marked difference between the two liquors.
Beer, which during the 'nineties, sold at the low price of 3d. or 4d.
a gallon was, of course, the daily drink of poor and middle-class people
alike [2] : ale, the price of which at the same period was normally 1s. 8d.
a gallon, was reserved by many for special occasions. If an employer
had to compensate his employees for work of special difficulty or for
overtime, or if, out of sheer goodwill, he wished to give them a treat,
he did so with ale or (as in the case of the workers employed at the
Mersey Mills) with notes payable in " Allowance Ale " at the *White
Bear* : beer, at 4d. a gallon, would be too tame and familiar to be
any reward at all. Sometimes the liquor was delivered for consumption off the premises, and was described as " Ale took out of Barr ",
at other times the record says " Ale took of Slate at the Barr " or simply
" off the slate ".

A striking feature of the accounts is the extent to which offsetting
of debts was effected. Customers were debited for malt and hops,
or ale and beer supplied to them, and credited for goods delivered
by them to Stubs ; so that, in some cases, no money had to pass, and

---

[1] Other professional men who were numbered among the customers
of Stubs were the Rev. M. Lloyd of Fairfield, the Rev. Mr. Lowe of
Winwick, Dr. Jackson, Mr. Shuttleworth, attorney, and Richard Willett,
schoolmaster of Hawarden.

[2] The price of " table beer " was the same as that of " beer ".

in others only a balance had to be settled, one way or the other, in bills or cash. This practice may be illustrated from the account of Thomas Watt. He was regularly debited with malt, hops, table beer and allowance ale for the men employed in his soap and candle business and on his flats on the river [1] ; on the other hand he was credited half-yearly with the rent due to him as lessor of the *White Bear*, as well as with candles and soap provided for Stubs. In the same way the malt supplied to Mrs. Heron went far towards covering the cost of the barley delivered by her to Stubs ; that taken by John Atherton, together with dung from Stubs' middins (valued in 1800 at 8s. 6d. a ton) helped to pay for the charcoal and coal provided by Atherton ; and the same was true of the payment to Robert Clough and John Pinnington who, also, supplied coal. Again, Ellen Johnson, who provided glasses and bottles for use at the *White Bear*, and Thomas Greaves of Mill Bank, who supplied paper for the packing of files, were paid largely in malt and hops. The principle of barter was explicitly laid down by a John Knowles who, on ordering an 18-gallon cask of ale in July, 1799, asked Stubs to reply saying what kind of groceries should be remitted in payment ; and other tradesmen paid their bills for malt and hops, partly at least, in wheat, beef, wines and spirits, potatoes, apples and onions. Similarly of services rendered to Stubs : the transport bills of Thomas Bradshaw and James Percy ; the cost of hiring a chaise or coach of Thomas Kay, when Stubs visited Liverpool on business or went to the races at Newton ; the rent of his seat in Church ; the rent by Stubs of a garden (at £3 a year) and " one years' hanging clothes in your Garden 14s. 6d." payable to Thomas Jackson ; even the fees in respect of his sons, at school with Richard Willett of Hawarden—all these were met in part or whole by malt, hops, ale, or beer supplied by Stubs.

The prices charged for malt and hops varied with the quality, and there were slight seasonal movements. But the figures on the opposite page, selected from a large number of individual entries in the Account Books, are representative of the charges made by Stubs to his customers.

From March, 1797, to April, 1798, the price of malt was steady at 7s. In May, 1798, it rose to 7s. 6d. and in October to 8s. Thereafter almost each successive month saw an increase, until a maximum of 15s. was reached in November, 1800. By May, 1801, the fall had set in, and in July, 1802, malt was again selling at a price of 8s. Generally the price of hops moved in the same direction as that of malt ; but in

---

[1] In the 13½ months between 14 November, 1795, and 26 January, 1797, he had 2,175½ quarts of ale from Stubs.

the crisis the percentage increase was greater, and after this was over the fall was more sudden and precipitous. Large movements in the prices of malt and hops affected those of ale, but beer (which was perhaps regarded as a mere by-product of ale) showed remarkable stability of price. In view of the place which beer occupied in the workers' budget this is a matter of some importance. For it suggests that index numbers of the cost of living which do not include beer may have led to a slight overestimate of the extent to which the standard of comfort of the poorer classes was pressed down during the last ten years of the eighteenth century.[1]

	Malt per measure.		Hops per lb.		Ale per gallon.		Beer per gallon.
	s. d.	s. d.	s. d.	s. d.	s. d.	s. d.	d.
1791 .	. 7 0		1 3		—		—
1792 .	. 7 4		1 1		1 8		—
1793 .	. 7 6		1 1		1 8		—
1794 .	. 7 6		1 0		1 8		3
1795 .	. 7 8		1 0–1	2	1 8		4
1796 .	. 8 4		1 3–2	0	1 10		4
1797 .	. 8 6–	7 0	2 0		1 10–1	8	4
1798 .	. 7 0		2 0–3	0	1 8		4
1799 .	. 7 0–	9 6	3 0–4	0	1 8–1	10	4
1800 .	. 10 0–15	0	3 0–2	7½	2 0–2	7	4
1801 .	. 14 0–11	0	2 0–1	0	2 6–2	0	4
1802 .	. 9 0–	7 6					

Of the purchase and sale of liquors other than those made of malt it is not necessary to say much. Wines and spirits never bulked large in the trade of the Inn, and supplies were generally obtained from local merchants. From 1789 onward Stubs bought port, brandy, gin, rum and cider of William Halsall of Warrington ; and among others who provided the same liquors, after 1792, were Edward Dakin of Warrington, and Kenwright & Shaw of Daresbury. (The bills payable to Edward Dakin, with whom dealings were most common, amounted to between £20 and £40 a year.) Only occasionally did Stubs look further afield. In 1791 he bought cider (at 14d. a gallon) of James Skey of Upton-upon-Severn ; in 1796 he ordered gin from Bristol, not only for himself but also for innkeepers in Manchester ; and in 1800, when (perhaps because of the high price of ale) his business in spirits was unusually large, he obtained a puncheon of " Fine Cordial

[1] Beer is not included in the 15 commodities on which Professor Silberling bases his index of the cost of living : according to his figures the cost of living rose from 97 in 1792 to 174 in 1801 (1790 = 100)— N. J. Silberling : *British Prices and Business Cycles, 1779–1850*.

Geneva " from Robert Castle & Co. of the same place. The records
are scanty ; but as far as they go they are indicative of rising prices
in the 'nineties.[1]

A minor source of profit to the *White Bear* was the sale of barm.
In March, 1798, a Liverpool firm of bakers, Dickins, King & Hurry
sent an order for regular supplies of 120 lb. to be delivered in two
consignments each week. They were bakers to the French Prison.
The price charged by Stubs was 3*d*. a pound, and between March and
July, barm to the value of £22 3*s*. was delivered to them. On 24
September, however, they wrote to say : " As we have done supplying
the French Prison, and we do not bake anything but Ship Bread, we
do not use any Barm at present." In November Joseph Jackson &
Sons of Liverpool, after having tried a sample, ordered 120 lb. a week
to be delivered " at twice ", and during the following four months
their purchases aggregated £22 12*s*. In October of the same year
Stubs began to supply three other Liverpool firms—those of Robert
Hastey, James Robinson and James Cooper. The accounts of the
first two of these were closed after a few weeks, but Cooper bought
30 lb. of barm a week for nearly two years. The price was normally
3*d*. a pound ; but by June, 1800, the shortage of barley had so reacted
on brewing, and hence on the supplies of yeast, that Stubs was able to
obtain as much as 8*d*. a pound from Cooper.

It would be easy to prolong this chapter by giving details of the
sources from which Stubs obtained the food and groceries—tea, coffee,
sugar, salt, cheese and so on—consumed at his inn. But they are of
no significance. Mention must, however, be made of his purchases
of the tumblers and bottles which were an important part of the
equipment of the *White Bear*. Warrington was a centre of glass
manufacture and Stubs was able to satisfy his needs from local sources.
In the years 1789–92 he obtained bottles and tumblers of Joshua Perrin,
Ellen Johnson, and John Unsworth—the last two of whom were relatives
of Stubs. In May, 1794, when Unsworth was in difficulties, he asked

---

[1] Rum, for example, cost 8*s*. a gallon in 1789, 10*s*. in 1792, 9*s*. 6*d*. in
1794, 11*s*. in 1795, 15*s*. in 1797 and 14*s*. in 1800. Gin or Geneva was
5*s*. in 1794, 5*s*. 6*d*. in 1795, 6*s*. in 1799, 7*s*. 6*d*. in 1800, 8*s*. 3*d*. in
1801 and 7*s*. in 1803. The corresponding prices for Cognac were :
1792, 14*s*., 1794, 16*s*., 1795, 15*s*., 1796, 18*s*., 1799, 17*s*., 1800, 18*s*–19*s*.,
and 1801, 19*s*.–24*s*. For Port they were : 1794, 7*s*. 6*d*., 1796, 9*s*.–11*s*.,
1800, 12*s*., 1801, 12*s*. Most of the wine and spirits was probably sold
in small quantities at the bar, but the Malt Account Books record an
occasional sale of rum or gin to customers in other places—to Mrs.
Twiss of Newton, Thomas Banner of Daresbury, Richard Shaw of
Daresbury, and so on.

Stubs for help in making an agreement with his creditors, " which will not only save me from entire ruin but make me into a man ", and offered to " sign over " everything to him. It is not unlikely, therefore, that Stubs acquired a financial interest in the concern, and that this explains why an Account Book and other documents of John Unsworth's (covering the years 1789–1803) is among the Stubs records. In May, 1800, Unsworth entered into an agreement of a kind not uncommon in the early days of steam-power industry : he arranged with a Thomas Carter to hire a room in Carter's warehouse in Oliver Street, Warrington, and to share the use of Carter's engine. He was to pay in rent £10 a year for each glass cutter or engraver employed by him, " and so in proportion for a greater or less time than a year " ; but Carter was to find coal for the engine and to keep it in repair. During the following two years Unsworth usually employed four hands in the room, but sometimes five or six : the accounts between the two were complicated, not only by this variation in the number of workers, but also by the allowances which Carter had to make whenever, even for a few hours, the engine was stopped for repairs.[1]

Notwithstanding his financial difficulties, John Unsworth seems to have built up an important connection. His invoice heading describes him as " Cut and Engrav'd Glass Manufacturer to his Majesty And to his Royal Highness, the Prince of Wales " ; and his account book shows that he supplied such well-known personages as Lord Stamford, Sir Richard Brooks, Sir Peter Warburton, Sir George Warren and Robert (afterwards Sir Robert) Peel with a wide variety of glass-ware— wine-glasses, goblets, cruets, decanters, girandoles, syllabub dishes, muffineer linings and so on. Among his customers were doctors, druggists, perfumiers, publicans and wine and spirit merchants in all parts of the country.

Stubs' own account in Unsworth's ledger records purchases from 1789 to 1799. In the first of these years he bought many dozens of ribbed half-pint tumblers, at 3s. 6d. a dozen, and a few dram glasses, at 2½d. each. By 1799 the price of the tumblers had risen to 4s. 6d. a dozen. At the same time Stubs bought glasses and quart wine-bottles (at 2s. 9d. a dozen) of Ellen Johnson. The invoices of both

[1] From July, 1803, to October, 1805, the accounts were between Unsworth and Ellen Carter, possibly the widow of Thomas Carter. The normal rent (expressed as a fee for turning the machinery for Unsworth) was now 22s. a week, and it would appear that four workmen were generally employed. A fee of 5s. 6d. a week was paid for each additional workman, and in those weeks when fewer than four hands were at work the rent was correspondingly reduced. Payment was made in cash at intervals of a week or two.

John Unsworth and Mrs. Johnson are for fairly large sums, and both made allowances on their bills for broken glass returned to them for remelting.[1]

A final sentence or two must be given to another aspect of Peter Stubs' activities at the inn. One of the functions of the publican of the eighteenth century was to provide a place where men of kindred interests could gather : there was a special " Soldiers' Room " at the *White Bear*. More important was that of providing a place of meeting for the clubs in which the industrial and provident aspirations of the poor found corporate expression. Many proprietors of public-houses themselves established " boxes " or funds out of which payments were made at times of sickness or death ; and innkeepers in one town would give information and help to those in another in such matters. Thus in November, 1791, John Harrop of the *Blue Bell Inn*, Manchester, asked Stubs to visit a member of his " Box " who had broken his leg through a fall from the coach in Warrington ; and in March, 1796, he wrote requesting Stubs to get from the captain of the recruiting party, lodged at the *Red Lion* in Bridge Street, a certificate of death of one John Burgess of the 39th regiment of foot (who had died at sea off Spike Island near the Cove of Cork), so that the widow might draw " the money that is allowed for ever soilder widow ". There is mention of the Box at the *White Bear* itself in a letter of September, 1793, from a John Davis, who had probably joined the club in Warrington and had afterwards removed to Manchester. It reads :

SIR, I receiv'd your note in August which was as follows Feb. 11—8d.,
$$s. \quad d. \qquad s. \qquad s. \quad d.$$
May 13—4 2, August 12—4, which is 8 – 10 Dr. to the Books by me which aforetime by John Golding expecting that he had paid it according to his promise which he had told me every time that he had paid the money, but as I am informed I am sorry to hear that he has proved [such] a Villian as to keep my money in his Custody, he always told me that he had paid it regular, but I hope if you will excuse me as I am innocent of his rogery, and I hope that you will stand my friend as to rectify the mistakes and that whatever I have to pay that you will answer for it or pass your word. If you please to give Mary Boardman a note after the next Club night of what I owe to the Box and I will immediately send the money or pay at Christmas as you please. I have sent
$$s. \quad d.$$
since last February 11 – 4. I will go to John Golding tomorrow to see whether he will pay it into your hands or not before the Club night.

Membership of the Box Club, it would seem likely, was not confined

---

[1] Corks for the bottles were bought of Ralph Nickson, at 1s. a gross. Puncheons, barrels and casks were supplied and repaired by a local cooper, Thomas Randle.

to the working-class. An invoice of Caldwell & Whitley, wholesale ironmongers of Warrington, includes an item " Over paid Club 13s.". It is just possible, however, that this relates to a contribution made on behalf of a workman, for it follows an entry, debited against Stubs, which reads " Paid T. Sutton when sick £1 10s.". The date of the invoice is of some interest : it is 11 May, 1804. It would appear that by this time Stubs had vacated the *White Bear* (perhaps to become the licensee of another inn, the *King's Head* [1]), for a printed set of rules dated 7 May, 1804, for a Sick Club which had its headquarters there gives the name of the landlord as Joseph Wright.[2] It seems possible that the items on the invoice of Caldwell & Whitley relate, therefore, to transactions arising out of the winding-up of the Box conducted by Stubs.

Light on the activities of the Box Club is disappointingly dim. But the glimmers that the records afford serve to remind us that the eighteenth-century inn was something more than a house of refreshment, and that it rendered some at least of the social services which, in a later day, are the province of such organs as the Friendly Societies, the Trade Unions and the State.

[1] A reference to repairs at the *King's Head* occurs in a plumber's bill of 1805, sent to Stubs.

[2] In the Warrington Public Library. The title is as follows : " Rules and Orders to be observed by a Society in the Parish of Warrington . . . for Raising and Supporting a Fund for the Maintenance of the Sick and Maimed Members and Burying their Dead : Held at the House of Mr. Joseph Wright, the Sign of the White Bear in Warrington aforesaid. Made and begun on the seventh day of May, 1804."

CHAPTER SEVEN

THE CARRIERS

NOT least among the factors that led to the success of Peter Stubs was the geographical situation of his business. Warrington had long been a nodal point in the road system of the north of England. Its position on the Mersey gave it access to supplies of material such as few other inland towns possessed ; and it was so placed that when, in the later decades of the eighteenth century, traffic was deflected from roads and rivers to the newly constructed canals it benefited, rather than lost, by the change. Its facilities for transport explain that diversity of economic activities which, as the preceding chapters have shown, was mirrored, in small, in the concern of Peter Stubs himself.

As early as 1774 the stage coaches from Liverpool to London were passing through Warrington twice daily on six days of the week : they were met there, on three days, by the coaches that went north, through Wigan, to Kendal. Stage coaches from Liverpool to Manchester travelled by Warrington three times a week in the summer months ; local coaches left Liverpool for Warrington and returned the same day four times a week ; and other coaches from Liverpool or Manchester gave almost daily communication with many of the larger towns of industrial England.[1] Although these vehicles were intended primarily for passengers who wished to travel quickly, they carried light parcels also ; and when customers of Stubs had urgent needs they sometimes sent instructions for their goods to be delivered by coach. On 16 May, 1793, for example, Thomas Richardson wrote to say that the Birmingham Fair would open in a week's time and that his files should therefore be sent by the Manchester coach instead of by waggon ; and in April, 1804, William Crooke, who mentioned that he was entirely without files, asked that his order should be sent immediately to Manchester and from there by the *Volunteer* coach to Burnley.

For the carriage of heavy goods coaches were never used : indeed, when in April, 1803, John Moseley of Covent Garden tried to send

[1] *Gore's Liverpool Directory*, 1774.

Stubs a " Gentlemen's Tool Chest ", the coach office in London refused to take it. And even for lighter goods transport by coach was rare, since the rates of carriage were high.[1] Generally the freight was paid by the customer. For trade with London, however, the practice was for the cost of carriage to be paid by the consignor, and customers in London were, therefore, less concerned than those in other places to find the cheapest form of transport. In February, 1805, a North-ampton client, Z. Rowton told Stubs to send his files by the Liverpool coach to London, and thence by the new Northampton coach, adding that he expected to be treated as a Londoner and have them carriage paid. Stubs managed, however, to find a better route. The *Royal Mail* from Manchester to London passed through Northampton and most subsequent deliveries to Rowton were made by this coach.

By far the greater part of the raw material and finished product of the file manufactory was carried by waggon. From Sheffield the rods of steel were brought to Stubs, for the most part, by a number of waggoners who travelled by way of Hathersage and Chapel-en-le-Frith. At Chapel two alternative routes offered themselves : the steel might be taken to Macclesfield and handed over to a carrier for trans-port to Warrington by road, or it might be taken to Manchester and left with the agent of the Duke of Bridgewater to send on by canal.[2] Between these alternatives Stubs seems to have alternated in choice according as, at particular times, one or the other proved cheaper or quicker.[3] In May, 1796, John Darwin wrote to say that carriage was less expensive by Macclesfield than by Manchester ; but in February, 1800, Walkers & Booth credited Stubs with excess carriage because the waggoner to whom they had given the steel had taken it by Maccles-field instead of the other way. After some correspondence with the carriers it was finally agreed that these might send it by whichever route they pleased, provided that the cost to Stubs was the same.

Several carriers shared the traffic. In 1787 there were three—Oliver, Hibberson and Goddard—plying regularly between Sheffield and Macclesfield or Manchester ; but within a few years the number

[1] In 1794 the charges from Manchester to London were 2s. 6d. for small parcels and 2d. per lb. for large ; to Warrington, a distance of 18 miles, they were 6d. for small parcels, and 6d. per stone for large. The passenger fare from Manchester to Warrington was 6s.—*Scholes's Manchester Directory*, 1794.

[2] From Sheffield to Manchester there was a choice of routes : the carrier sometimes found it more convenient to bring the steel by Barnsley, Penistone, Mottram and Ashton-under-Lyne.

[3] In 1787 it took the waggons two and a half days to travel from Sheffield to Manchester.

G

had grown considerably, and parcels of steel were, at one time or another, carried by Johnson, Kirk & Lomas, Moss, Lomas & Thompson, and Woodward, as well as by those already mentioned.[1] Most of these transport concerns were small family businesses [2] or partnerships conducted by men whose homes were at places intermediate between the terminals of their journey : a letter of May, 1792, from John Harrison informed Stubs that " the Carriers Johnson and Gothard [sic] keep their books at either Manchester or their own House on ye road ". Supervision of men and horses was probably easier from a half-way point, since goods were not taken through by a single waggoner but by relays : at Chapel-en-le-Frith the waggoner from Sheffield handed over the goods to another man, employed by the same concern, who took them on to Macclesfield, where they were delivered to an independent carrier. In the early days of Stubs' business two men, George Howard and George Lomas, seem to have shared the work of bringing the steel from Macclesfield to Warrington, but in the later years a single carrier, Randal Walton, performed this service.

If, in other branches of trade, evidence has been found of partial monopoly, in road transport there is little sign of anything but pure competition ; and rivalry, indeed, was so keen that the carriers sometimes overstepped the bounds of honesty in their scramble for business. In April, 1793, John Lomas wrote to say that James Goddard had been to Harrison & Son's works " and fetcht 5 cwt. of Steele in our name and I sopose he tooke it to Manchester ". In 1795 Kirk & Lomas told John Harrison that Peter Stubs had ordered the whole of his steel to be sent by their waggons, and Lomas & Thompson also told him that they had been given the exclusive rights to the same traffic. In December, 1802, a veritable traffic war developed. Robert Moss & Co. wrote to say that Hibberson had promised to have them off the road or to carry for nothing ; and they, in turn, declared that they would " charge as little as Hibberson, let them charge as little as they will . . . as we are a few young men who have Families and have a hard world to fight against ". (There is no evidence, however, that competition

---

[1] *Scholes's Manchester Directory*, 1794, gives Robert Hibberson, John Johnson and James Goddard as the carriers to Sheffield ; *Robinson's Sheffield Directory*, 1797, contains the names of Kirk & Lomas, Hibberson, Goddard and Johnson, as carriers to Manchester or Macclesfield.

[2] Evidence of the family concern appears in the following from the *Sheffield Iris* of 14 June, 1793. " On Tuesday last, a son of Mr. Hibberson, one of the Manchester carriers from this place, fell from the shafts of a waggon he was driving near Baslow . . . and the wheels running over his neck severed his head from his body."

went to the extremes it did in the case of a Sheffield coach-proprietor, Mr. Peach of the *Angel Inn*, of whom it was said that when rival coach-owners carried passengers to London for nothing, not only did he do the same but also gave each passenger a bottle of wine as a reward for patronizing him.[1])   It should be added that Robert Moss subsequently showed himself no more tolerant of newcomers to the business than Hibberson had been with him : " I have some reason to think ", he wrote in August, 1804, " that Jas. Loman [sic] (the man I imploy from Chapel to Maxfd.) is in a very sly way going to suplant me as far as he can.   Should application be made to you for any alteration in delivering of the goods at Sheffd. hope you will take no notice of it but let them come as usual & you may depend on the greatest care and punctuality."   Though it was never the policy of Stubs to give the whole of his custom to any one concern with which he had dealings, he apparently complied with this request, and Moss & Co. continued to enjoy a large share of his traffic to and from Sheffield.

In the early years there seems to have been no definite arrangement as to whether the carrier from Sheffield should be paid by the consignor or by Stubs.   In May, 1792, John Harrison wrote, " Am sorry our people have been so remis about ye Car^g. but as it is a thing we are not accustomed to paying, they frequently forget . . . as we have had no Carriers' Bills in since Christmas, therefore we can't ascertain how much we shall be charg^d with, therefore wish you would take notice what you do pay and we shall be always ready to allow it."   Such uncertainty was unbusinesslike, and shortly afterwards it became the practice for Harrison and the other factors to pay the Sheffield carrier for transporting the steel to Macclesfield or Manchester, and for Stubs to pay the carrier who brought it on to Warrington.   In 1801, however, Stubs asked that henceforth payment of carriage over the whole journey should be left to him : the carrier who took over the steel at Macclesfield or Manchester paid the bill of the man who had brought it from Sheffield and included this as an item in the account he presented to Stubs.

These changes of practice make it difficult to trace the variations of transport costs over the whole period.   But the chief movements are plain.   In 1793 and 1794 a Thomas Bradshaw, whose home was at Sparrow Pit, near Chapel-en-le-Frith, brought steel all the way from Sheffield to Warrington at a rate of 2s. 9d. per cwt. ; and in 1795 and 1796 another waggoner, John Thompson, did the same for 2s. 7d. per cwt.   When, as more usually happened, two carriers shared the work, the bills indicate that the charge from Sheffield to Macclesfield

---

[1] *The Songs of Joseph Mather* 82 n.

was 1s. 9d. and that on to Warrington 1s. per cwt., until 1799. In that year rates were increased, and by March, 1800, the charge from Sheffield to Macclesfield had reached 2s. 6d. To what extent the rate from Macclesfield to Warrington also increased in 1800 there is no means of knowing, but in 1806 the Macclesfield carrier, Randal Walton, was charging 1s. 2d. per cwt. for his services.

Carriage to Manchester was somewhat more costly than to Maccles-field : in 1792 it was 2s., and between 1793 and 1799 2s. 6d. per cwt. Thereafter a sharp upward movement occurred : by September, 1800, the charge was 3s. 6d. ; and this rate persisted till March of the follow-ing year, when John Harrison, Eyre, Hall & Smith and other factors succeeded in getting it reduced to 3s.—though less regular clients of the carriers (such as Huntsman & Sons) were still charged 3s. 6d. and even 3s. 9d. By October, 1801, the rate had come down to 2s. 9d. ; in 1803 it was 2s. 8d. ; and in 1804 Moss & Co. were again delivering steel for Stubs at Manchester at the normal price of the 'nineties, 2s. 6d.[1]

The high rate to Manchester, as compared with that to Macclesfield, was offset by the low cost of carriage by canal from Manchester to Warrington. The rate charged by the Duke of Bridgewater for this journey was only 3d. per cwt. from 1793 to 1799, and even in the infla-tion of 1800 and 1801 it was only 4d. It was important, however, that when steel was sent to Manchester, instructions as to the manner of forwarding from there should be explicit : more than once the Sheffield factors had to compensate Stubs for a substantial difference of freight when parcels of steel were inadvertently handed over to a road carrier at Manchester, instead of to the agent of the canal.[2]

[1] For whatever reason, the carriage debited to Stubs by Walkers & Booth of Rotherham was always less than that debited by the Sheffield factors, though there is evidence that the steel was carried from Rother-ham through Sheffield. From February, 1798, when the first consign-ment was made, to June, 1799, the rate from Rotherham to Manchester was 2s. It was then raised to 2s. 2d., and in February, 1800, to 2s. 9d. This last was the rate charged throughout 1800 and the early months of 1801 when the Sheffield factors were paying 3s. 6d. The disparity was not unobserved by Stubs, and, in March, 1801, he suggested to his friends that they should look into the matter. Hibberson, the carrier, assured Eyre, Hall & Smith that they had charged Walkers & Booth 3s. per cwt. since April, 1800. If Hibberson was speaking the truth, Walkers & Booth must have been asking Stubs less than they were charged, for 2s. 9d. is invariably the rate on their invoices through-out these months.

[2] In the rare instances in which steel was sent by the Old Navigation— the Mersey and Irwell—the rate was the same as by canal.

For the transport of steel to his outworkers, Stubs again made use of the services of public carriers by road. A local waggoner, Catterall, made regular deliveries to Peter Whitfield and James Plumpton at Ditton ; a carter, Nield, took supplies to James Lyon at Stockport : and steel sent to Carolus Charles was carried by Henshall, Marsh or Sherwood to Liverpool and thence by another carrier to Aughton—though sometimes, to save carriage, Charles intercepted the waggon at Prescot. Waggoners also played the principal part in the transport of files to customers in all parts of the kingdom. The Sheffield carriers who brought steel returned with parcels for delivery at places on their route or for forwarding to customers in Nottingham, Gainsborough and so on. The waggons of James Lawrinson and Henry Marsh, which passed daily through Warrington on their way between Liverpool and Manchester, carried boxes and parcels of files on the first stage of their journey to many places. A carrier, Hargreaves, travelled to Kendal ; another, Morris, delivered goods to Nantwich, the Potteries and South Staffordshire ; yet another, Kirk, made short journeys through Wigan to the more northerly parts of Lancashire.

Most of the names mentioned above are those of men who operated transport services over only a relatively small area. When parcels were sent any great distance they had to pass through the hands of a whole chain of such carriers ; and even such a short journey as that from Warrington to Skipton might involve the services of at least three different firms of carriers. In September, 1792,. Abraham Chamberlain complained that a parcel of files sent to him there had got wet and asked Stubs to join him in suing the carrier. He added that the man who received them at Wigan almost always used open carts, and he therefore asked that future consignments should be sent by way of Manchester and Halifax. Some months later, however, in April, 1794, he instructed Stubs to send his goods to Wigan again, to be forwarded from there by a Mr. Wraith to Blackburn, where they could be handed over to a third carrier who would bring them to Skipton.

When, as in this case, goods were damaged, or when, as frequently happened, they suffered delay it was not always easy to allocate responsibility. In May, 1800, William Gawthorpe of Kendal wrote asking Stubs to make inquiries about a hamper of hardware, which had disappeared. It had been sent by water from Birmingham to Stockton Quay, where it had been handed over to Robert Kirk, the Warrington carrier ; and a carter from Lancaster had said that he had seen such a hamper " laying in a Cellar, under old St. Simon's Stable, Lancaster, all plunder'd Excepting a few wire mousetraps ". According to Gawthorpe, the hamper had been rifled at Preston when in the custody of Kirk, and Stubs was asked to look into the matter. Apparently Kirk was not able to deny responsibility. In June Gawthorpe paid an account owing to Stubs by a bill on Kirk for ten guineas (which, no doubt, represented the compensation he had obtained) and said that he blamed Kirk for concealing the hamper after it had been robbed. A somewhat similar case occurred in November, 1804, when Charles Tuckley of Coleshill, Warwickshire, wrote to say he had not received the files Stubs had directed to him and that he had made inquiries of both the carriers concerned. " Gray says he never saw the files and Dann says they never was in his waggon. . . . I have told them both you will make one of them pay for them ", he added, " and I hope you will for Gray bears but a very poor Carrackter." Yet again, in February, 1805, Moss & Co., the Sheffield carriers, wrote to say that Longden & Co. had charged them 30s. for goods that had been damaged on their way to Warrington. He suggested that Randal Walton, the Macclesfield carrier, ought to pay part of it, " as it's not known were they were damaged. The box seemed in good order when del^d to them and in that case it is rather hard we should be at all the loss."

Troubles such as these could be avoided when a single carrier was able to take care of the goods from start to finish. For his large market in the Midlands Stubs was able to make use of the widespread under-taking of John Twiss, whose waggons travelled over an area including Lancaster, Manchester, Liverpool, Birmingham and London.[1] A still larger concern which operated an almost national service was that of Pickfords' : their waggons and fly-boats were to be seen in all parts ; and some indication of the size of their enterprise is given by the offer they made, in 1803, to supply 400 horses, 50 waggons and 28 boats for the use of the Government.[2] They carried for Stubs on both short and long routes, as is shown by many bills of freight ; and the absence of correspondence with them may be taken as negative evidence of their efficiency.

If Peter Stubs had reasonably good facilities for transport by road he was even better provided with those for transport by water. A short distance from his workshops were Bank Quay and Howley Quay, from which flats sailed on the Mersey and Irwell Navigation, to Manchester, on the one hand, and to Runcorn and Liverpool on the

---

[1] For the services of John Twiss see *Scholes's Manchester and Salford Directory*, 1794, and *Chapman's Birmingham Directory*, 1801.

[2] *Sheffield Iris*, 14 July, 1803.

other.[1] A little further away, to the south, were Stockton Quay and London Bridge, from which barges on the Duke of Bridgewater's Canal took goods, east to Castlefield, Manchester, and west to Preston Brook, where the Duke's navigation joined the Trent and Mersey (or Grand Trunk) Canal which had its terminus at Runcorn. By the Trent and Mersey vessels passed through the salt area of Cheshire and the Potteries to Burton and Wilden Ferry, where the River Trent gave access to Gainsborough and the Humber. At Fradley the Trent and Mersey joined the Coventry Canal ; and at Fazeley, near Tamworth, this in turn was linked with the Birmingham navigations. Near Haywood, the Trent and Mersey met the Staffordshire and Worcestershire Canal, which led by Stourport to the Severn and so to Bristol. By these navigations, then, Warrington was connected with the sea at the important ports of Liverpool, Hull and Bristol.

Nor was this all. A short distance to the west of Warrington was Sankey Bridge, where goods could be put on vessels plying on the Sankey Navigation, past Newton, to St. Helens. Communication by water with growing industrial areas was given by the Rochdale Canal (and other canals) which joined the Bridgewater at Manchester. And a short journey from Warrington to Wigan by land enabled Stubs to make use, if he wished, of the Liverpool and Leeds Canal, only part of which, however, was yet in operation, as well as of the Douglas Navigation.

As a private individual the Duke of Bridgewater was able to act as a public carrier and to collect payment for freight as well as tolls on his canal. The other canals, however, were owned by companies, and, since a company was not allowed to act as a public carrier, goods were transported on boats owned by individuals or small partnerships. Chief among these (so far as the dealings of Stubs are concerned) were Hugh Henshall & Co., Worthington & Gilbert, and Thomas & James Pickford. The vessels of all three left Castle Quay, Manchester, daily, calling at Stockton Quay, near Warrington, to pick up goods for such important centres as Coventry and Birmingham ; and from Coventry Pickfords' forwarded these either by water or by fly-waggon to London and beyond. In the other direction the canal carriers loaded cargoes of barley or hops at such inland ports or transhipment centres as Stourport, Fazeley, and Shardlow [2] and brought them to

[1] From 1801, when the Old Quay Canal was cut, vessels were able to pass from Runcorn to Warrington without having to wait for the tide, as they had formerly had to do when they passed along the river itself.

[2] Shardlow is situated about 6 miles from Derby, at the junction of the Trent and Mersey Canal with the River Trent.

Warrington. Other carriers employed frequently by Stubs were J. & G. Ames, who plied between Bristol and Stourport, Adam Southern & Co., who carried from Stourport to Stockton Quay, and Sampson Newill, whose headquarters were at Stoke. A printed notice of the last of these dated 14 May, 1794, indicates that his fly-boats left the Potteries twice a week for Branston, near Daventry, where the Oxford Canal joined the Grand Junction, and from which point goods were sent on to all parts of Northamptonshire as well as to London. A letter from Newill shows that he was willing to combine his work as carrier with that of a buyer of grain on commission ; and a similar combination of function is found in the case of Ward & Holland of Oxford, who sold barley to Stubs in the years 1802–5 and sent it in their own boats from Oxford to Stockton Quay.

The inland navigations were used chiefly for transport of heavy and bulky goods. As already mentioned, steel from Sheffield or Rotherham was frequently carried on the last stage of its journey from Manchester by the Bridgewater Canal. That from the Calder Iron Company was put on board vessels at Greenock, brought by sea to Liverpool, and carried from there by flats on the Mersey Navigation. Occasional consignments from Newcastle-upon-Tyne came by packet boat to Gainsborough and thence by the Trent and Mersey and Bridgewater canals. And steel from the Brades works in Birmingham was brought the whole way by inland navigation. Barley, bought through dealers in Liverpool, was sent by the Navigation direct to Bank Quay or Howley Quay : that bought through the merchants or commission dealers in other parts of the country was put in bags by the farmers, carried to the wharves and sent by canal to Stockton Quay,[1] where it was delivered to the agent of the Duke of Bridgewater, James Percy,[2] who paid the carrier's bill, warehoused the grain, and sent in his account for the whole to Stubs. Charges for landing, loading into carts and bringing to Warrington were paid by Stubs to local carriers, such as

---

[1] In a letter concerning the carriage of 15½ tons of barley which Stubs had bought of A. P. Sharp of Rugeley, Sampson Newill, the carrier, wrote : " I sent this Boat light from the Pottery to Fazeley on purpose, and when we arrived there, they Farmers had not brought it down to the wharf, therefore in Course we had to tramp Country round. Mr. Sharp wrote to me to say it was ready but found to the Contrary. The business was attended with a great deal of Trouble and Expense and am afraid will throw this Boat out of its regular time going to Branston to meet they waggons. If so they Carrier will make me pay all the Expenses on 30 Horses for the time they lay in waiting for the Boat."

[2] In later years, J. Goulden.

R. Higginson, George Short, Thomas Longshaw, Thomas Leigh and James Tickle.

Malt and beer were carried from Warrington to customers in Liverpool and Manchester by either the canal or the " Old Navigation ". Files also, when there was no urgency for delivery, were frequently sent to customers in the Midlands and the Severn Valley by water : boxes consigned to the Coalbrookdale Co. went by canal to Stourport and thence by trow up the Severn ; those to James Dowell of Bristol either to Stourport by water, or Bewdley by land, and thence down the Severn. Occasionally, however, it was found cheaper to send goods to Bristol by sea from Liverpool ; and sea transport played an important part in the carriage to other centres also. The Glasgow houses usually instructed Stubs to send their goods to an agent in Liverpool who put them on board vessels for the Clyde : on one occasion Archibald Turner complained that files which had been sent him by road had cost 23s. for transport, as against the 3s. or 4s. they would have cost by water, and he therefore said he expected Stubs to pay half this charge. The Carron partners also ordered their files to be sent to Liverpool, whence their warehouseman would send them on by their own boats ; and William and Edward Perry of Whitehaven similarly had their orders sent on by sea from Liverpool. In 1801 an Exeter customer, Samuel Jesse, asked that his files should be sent by a clay vessel from Liverpool (with unfortunate results, for the files were wet and spoilt when they arrived). And in 1805 when Stubs had to deliver goods to Walter Miller of Perth he was advised to send them by road to Newcastle, or by road to Leeds, canal to Hull, and thence by sea to Dundee.

Costs of carriage by water were relatively low. The rates charged by the Duke of Bridgewater for bringing steel from Manchester to Stockton Quay were 5s. 2d. a ton from 1793 to 1799 and 6s. 8d. a ton thereafter. Six bundles of steel were brought by vessel from Greenock to Liverpool in July, 1803, at a cost of 2s. 10d. ; and although cartage to warehouse and warehouse charges added 1s. 8d., and Custom House and agency charges 1s. 6d., the total expenses were only 6s., or about 1s. per cwt. Unfortunately the bills of the carriers on the Trent and Mersey and other canals do not often specify the point from which the goods were shipped. But a letter of Sampson Newill of 1796 shows that he charged 23s. a ton for carrying barley from Fazeley to Stockton Quay—although, according to Newill's statement, the charge by Henshall's boats for the same service was 25s. Another from Caparn, Barber & Hare indicate that the cost of carriage of malt from Shardlow to Stockton Quay was 22s. a ton in 1803 and 1804. And a bill of John Wayte, carrier, of Stoke, gives the charge on barley from Stour-

port to Stockton Quay in 1802 as 32s. 6d. per ton.   Hops were carried
by Worthington & Gilbert by canal from Worcestershire for 2s. per
cwt. in 1794 and 1795, 2s. 9d. in 1798, and 3s. in 1801.   In 1806 the
charges on a box brought from Bristol by the same carrier were at the
rate of 38s. 8d. a ton, and another carrier, J. & G. Ames, charged 33s. 6d.
a ton on spirits brought from the same place in the same year.   Whether
or not rates included tonnage payable to the canal companies is not
shown.   The canal dues, however, were quite low : a bill of 1799
shows that those from Fradley to Preston Brook, payable to the
proprietors of the Trent and Mersey, were only 3s. 8d. per ton.

Since freight bills on files and tools were almost always paid by the
consignee there is no means of ascertaining the charges on goods sent
away from Warrington by water ; but letters from customers give
some indication of their level compared with those of the road carriers.
They show, moreover, that, as road rates increased in the last years
of the eighteenth century, there was a growing tendency on the part
of customers to have their goods sent by canal.   In February, 1799,
for example, Warham, Potts & Smith of Leeds asked that henceforth
their files should be sent by canal as far as Manchester : " We used to
have hinges ", they said, " from Ashton, until the price of Carriage
came to be so excessively high.   The files which we have from you
cost us 8d. per stone."   In January, 1802, George Lewis of Birmingham wrote, " You did sadly wrong in sending . . . by land, for the
carriage was near 8s, which takes all the Gold of the Ginger Bread."
In November, 1805, Edward Reynolds of Coventry, who for several
years had been accustomed to receive files by Pickfords' boats, complained that Stubs had sent a parcel by Twiss's waggon and that he
had had to pay 8s. 6d., as against the charge of 2s. 6d. by boat.   And
in December of the same year, Cox & Weatherhead of Derby asked
that their order should be sent by the boats of Henshall & Co. or
Sorsby & Black, adding, " The last box we had from you went thro'
Sheffield and we never have less to pay than 1d. per lb. carriage for any
[of] your goods." [1]

---

[1] Incidentally, the rising cost of road transport was affecting postal
rates, and customers began to ask that the invoices should be put in
the parcels or boxes with the files.   In May, 1796, Thomas Richardson
of Birmingham remarked that to send the bill of parcels by post was
" like throwing 5d. away " : in the following year Gawthorpe & Berry
of Kendal asked to have their invoice with the files " as postage is now
become very expensive " ; and in January, 1802, Archibald Turner of
Glasgow protested that he had been charged 2s. 3d. postage on the last
invoice " on account of so much strong paper in it ".

It is probable that carriage by road was more speedy than that by canal—though in 1805 Edward Reynolds of Coventry said he received files by boat as quickly as by waggon—and it was certainly more reliable, for rivers and canals might suffer from drought, frost, or other obstructions to transport. In April, 1797, J. & G. Lewis of Birmingham asked that their goods should be sent by waggon, since the canal was about to be closed for repairs, and in September, 1799, they mentioned that the canal had been out of action owing to floods. In October, 1803, J. Orton of Polesworth wrote that, owing to drought, the boat would not carry more than 70 or 80 quarters of barley, " which is the same expense as 100 Qrs. except tonnage ". In January, 1803, Ward & Holland of Oxford were unable to send a cargo of barley because the frost would not allow the boats to pass, and in December, 1805, Wright & Hazelhurst mentioned that there had been delay in sending a parcel of slates because " the Staffordshire Canal as been stopt with Ice ". The frequency of frost was such, indeed, that some of the canal carriers had notes printed ready to send to their customers to explain any delay that might arise from this cause. Impediments arising from the weather were not, however, confined to water transport : on 15 February, 1805, Moss, the Sheffield carrier, informed Stubs that he had had 70 tons of goods held up " just in the American time of sending ", and that he had been unable to get over the moors from Sheffield for a fortnight.[1]

The correspondence of customers with Stubs indicates an attitude of suspicion towards the carriers, whether by road or water ; and these were frequently accused of making excessive charges and of other malpractice. As already mentioned, it was usual for freight to be paid on delivery, but in May, 1802, the Sheffield Quaker, Daniel Doncaster, wrote to say he had paid the carriage on a parcel of Sheffield files he had sent, in order " to prevent imposition which is commonly the case with carriers ". Waggoners, " steerers " and flatmen were, no doubt, usually rough in their methods and not always scrupulous in their sense of property ; and precautions had to be taken against theft. When money was to be sent to him by the Liverpool carriers, Carolus Charles asked that it should be made up in a parcel that could not be opened ; and when in April, 1796, John Clayton of Manchester ordered a barrel of ale to be sent by the Old Navigation, he asked that

---

[1] Joseph Wood, at this time on a journey for Stubs in Yorkshire, also mentioned the bad weather. " I never had so rough a passage over Blackstone edge before ", he wrote from Tadcaster on 2 February, " I have been in Perils by Frost, in Perils by Snow and up to the middle in Snow Drifts often."

it should be put at the bottom of the Market Boat " so that it shall be well stow'd from the men ". Fears were expressed lest malt should disappear on the way : " Could not the gross weight of the Malt & Sacks be taken ? " asked Edward Kearsley of Hulton in March, 1804, " I am sure aforetime we had not the quantity of malt that you allow. This I mean to prevent theft on the road." Nor was it only the clients of the carriers who might suffer from the predatory instincts of the waggoners : " Always see the Goods sent to us enter'd in the way Bill ", wrote T. & J. Newby of Kendal in June, 1792. " We observe the driver deprives his Master of the Carriage."

It would be wrong, however, to lay much stress on the defects of either the means of transport themselves or the men who operated them. Writers of the Victorian era, anxious to set in high relief the achievements of the locomotive, paid perhaps too much attention to the disadvantages of a transport system which made no use of the iron rail and of steam power. Their writings colour our impressions to-day. For what it is worth, the opinion may be hazarded that the technique of transport, in the period we are concerned with, did not lag far behind the technique of manufacture ; that enterprise was not lacking ; and that Peter Stubs, at least, was not ill served by those who carried his goods.

CHAPTER EIGHT

THE MEDIUM OF EXCHANGE

I

In the history of a business undertaking of the twentieth century there would be no chapter with this heading. The existence of an adequate supply of legal tender money and of a system of bank deposits transferable by cheque would be taken for granted. But in the days of Peter Stubs a manufacturer could never be quite certain of getting cash for the payment of wages ; and the instruments by which purchasing power was normally transferred from one person and place to another frequently operated with a good deal of friction and sometimes failed to work at all. It has already been suggested that the difficulty and expense of transferring currency or credit was one of the reasons for the existence of barter in the relations between Stubs and the Sheffield steel-makers. Traces of similar practice can be found in those between Stubs and others—as, for example, James Sword of Glasgow, who in 1792 sent two casks of Turkey oil-stones, valued at £13 16s., asking Stubs to dispose of them as best he could and credit Sword's account. Generally, however, some media of exchange entered into the dealings and it is the purpose of this chapter to consider the nature of these.

Small orders had usually to be paid for in cash. Where the customer lived at a distance from Warrington he would sometimes ask to be allowed to defer payment till he had occasion to visit the town. Thus, in June, 1792, a Macclesfield customer, Needham, requested Stubs to have his account ready for Friday night when he would call to pay it ; and in April, 1793, J. Lewis (of Lewis & Vaughan of Birmingham) when sending a small order, mentioned that he would be in Warrington at Midsummer and would make payment then. Sometimes—and especially in the case of customers in Manchester—money was sent by a public carrier. On 28 June, 1792, John Brown of the *Nag's Head*, Manchester, sent 2 guineas by the waggoner, and on the same day James Faulkner, a timber-merchant of the same town, sent 4 guineas by the coachman. Again, in October, 1794, James Sibbald, a joiner, of Manchester, wrote, " This morning at Eight Cloack Paid to Captain

Kay belonging to his Greace the Duck of Bridge Waters Pleaser boat
£2 – 12 – 8 . . . which you will receive from Mr. James Perce
[Percy] Book Keeper to the Duck, London bridg." It was not always
safe, however, to entrust cash to the hands of a waggoner or flatman :
it was often better to enclose it in a parcel of goods, so that the carrier
knew nothing about it. As already mentioned, on one occasion Carolus
Charles asked Stubs to hide the guineas he was to send in straw in a
box ; and in 1805 Andrew Lees, a gunsmith of Wednesbury, sent
" inclosed in a bit of wood 4 Bank of England Bills, half a guinea, one
shilling, and three sixpences, making £4 – 13s.".

Sometimes a man who had payment to make would ask to be allowed
to wait until Stubs, or a representative of Stubs, called for it : in the
later years of the concern it was one of the chief tasks of Joseph Wood
to collect money in this way. Sometimes the services of commercial
travellers employed by others were enlisted. " I will pay you the
money by Mr. Leigh's outrider when he comes to Leek ", wrote
William Ash in May, 1797 ; and in April, 1803, Robert Webster of
Shrewsbury announced that he was sending £13 15s. through a traveller
employed by Joseph Tarratt of Wolverhampton.

Among the itinerant traders who could serve in this way were
dealers in cattle. In some parts of Wales, merchants who had money
to pay in London found it convenient to give cash to the drovers,
with instructions to hand it over to their creditors. The drovers,
however, soon found it better to leave the money at home and to pay
the creditors out of the proceeds of the sale of their cattle. In this
way they came to exercise one of the functions of a banker, and it was
through such transactions that the Llandovery Bank and the Aberyst-
wyth and Tregaron Bank came into being—the former known as the
Bank of the Black Ox and the latter as the Bank of the Black Sheep.[1]
In industrial Lancashire cattle drovers played a less important part in
economic life than in Wales. But that dealers who travelled to the
grazing areas were sometimes employed to effect remittances is shown
by a letter of November, 1790, in which a customer in Settle wrote,
" You may send for pay by some of your Butchers that attends our
Fairs." [2]

Payments could, of course, be made through the medium of the
Post Office : in February, 1795, Roger Lewis was credited with 6

---

[1] S. E. Thomas : *The Rise and Growth of Joint Stock Banking*,
Vol. I, 46 n.

[2] In November, 1802, J. Yates of Manchester sent a man to Warrington
Fair to sell a horse, with directions to hand the money he received
to Stubs, who was to credit the account of Travis & Yates accordingly.

guineas sent in cash by the post woman, and in December, 1796, James Newton of Newark sent a draft for 5 guineas through the Post. But the cost was inordinately high. When sending a bill on London for £6 1s., in December, 1794, Thomas Kirkup of Sunderland remarked that he would have transmitted by the Post Office but found that the cost would have been 3s. 8d. ; and in January of the same year Jacob Butler of Birmingham mentioned that he had been to the Post Office to remit the balance of his account to Stubs, but was told he would have to pay 8d. per £ in addition to the stamp. He therefore asked if there was any Warrington tradesman who did business in Birmingham to whom he could pay the sum due.

Three-cornered transactions of the kind just suggested were, in fact, very common. In February, 1792, Abraham Chamberlain of Skipton sent a letter authorizing Stubs to receive the sum of £20 0s. 6d. from four persons in Warrington and Ashton-in-Makerfield ; and in May of the same year he wrote, " You'll please to receive the money from Jackson—also 4 guineas from Mr. Harrison." William Ash of Leek promised to pay his bill for files in August, 1791, through a Mr. Leigh, grocer of Warrington. Thomas Harding of Ashley Heath informed Stubs, in January, 1793, that he had written to Messrs. Hall & Randle, coopers, and Mr. Crompton, blacksmith, to pay for the files Stubs had sent him. And James Faulkner of Manchester wrote in July, 1800, to say he had " sent £1 16s. 6d. work done for Mr. Wood, Cabinet Maker, Bridge St." and had told him to take the money to Stubs and ask Stubs to send a gross and a half of files. Instances of this kind might be multiplied. But one more will suffice. In January, 1791, John Salt of Stafford wrote : " I have this day remitted to Thomas Lyon & Co. wherein, I requested them to pay you Two pounds two shillings and sixpence the whole of your Accompt. Am sorry it has been so long but it has been oweing to Lyon & Cos not having done any business since April last till within about a month ago or I should have got them to a Pay'd you sooner." Possibly the infrequency of business with Lyon led Salt to look elsewhere, for a letter of August, 1792, shows that he was then carrying out his financial operations through a Warrington soap-boiler : " If you don't send the files ", he wrote, " I must get my correspondent Mr. Thos. Watt to pay you the balance."

The intermediary in such transactions was not always resident in Warrington. In March, 1791, John Broom & Son asked Stubs if he had a friend in Bristol whom they could pay ; in March of the following year James Horrocks of Leek wrote, " Mr. Mould of Longnor told me he paid someone at Congleton for you. If you please to inform me who I must pay . . . can do it almost any day as Congleton is only 10 Mile from us "; and in May, 1797, Thomas Jepson of Lincoln wrote, " When I have occasion for anything more in your way and it is agreeable to you I can in future pay the money to Mr. Blundell of this Town who I understand has some dealings with you in the Corn Trade."

Through whatever channel they were made most of the smaller payments were in the form of coin. Mention has already been made of guineas sent by way of public carriers, and there are references to payments in gold in letters from Reginald Owen of Croft in 1799, from Robert Patterson of Belfast in 1800, and from Andrew Lees of Wednesbury in 1805—long after the suspension of cash payments by the Bank of England.[1] Under an Act of 1777 the circulation of bank notes of less than £5 had been virtually prohibited. After the crisis of 1797, however, the Bank of England issued notes of £1 and £2 and the private banks were again permitted to put out notes of small denomination.[2] But there were few note-issuing banks in Lancashire, and notes of country banks in other areas would hardly be accepted there; though in July, 1797, Mark Gilpin of the Coalbrookdale Iron Company paid Stubs in Shrewsbury and Wellington bank notes, and in November, 1799, John Highway of Shrewsbury sent a " Broasley five guinea Bill No. 447 "—probably a note of a bank set up by the iron-master, John Wilkinson. Bank of England notes had a wider currency ; but, as is well known, Lancashire traders of this period looked with distaste on notes of any kind, not only because, since these were payable to bearer, there was danger of theft,[3] but also because of a long experience of over-issues and failures of note-issuing banks in all parts of England.

II

By far the most common means of payment between traders at this period was the bill of exchange. " Bills, since they circulate chiefly

---

[1] The payment from Belfast was made through John Chorley, perhaps when he was returning from a visit there. That it should have been made in gold is not a matter for surprise, for gold remained the medium of exchange in the North of Ireland long after notes had largely taken its place in England and southern Ireland. *See Note on the State of the Exchange between London and Dublin from 1797 to 1804* in McCulloch's *Select Collection of Tracts on Paper Currency and Banking* (1857), 346.

[2] A. E. Feavearyear : *The Pound Sterling*, 171.

[3] " The sum which I owe being small I will endeavour to get a Bill to the amount . . . as I don't like to remit Bank notes payable only to bearer ", wrote James Newton of Newark in July, 1794.

among the trading world, come little under the observation of the public ", wrote Henry Thornton in 1802. " The amount of bills in existence may yet, perhaps, be at all times greater than the amount of all the bank notes of every kind, and of all the circulating guineas." Lancashire was especially addicted to their use. " Liverpool and Manchester ", Thornton added in a footnote, " effect the whole of their larger mercantile payments not by country bank notes, of which none are issued by the banks of those places, but by bills of one or two months date, drawn on London." [1] Other economists, at a later period, wrote to the same effect. In giving evidence before the Committee on Banks of Issue in 1840, S. J. Loyd said that bills of exchange circulating in Lancashire " bore a proportion as ten to one or more to the gold and Bank of England notes " ; [2] and John Fullarton remarked in 1845 that bills had been employed " during a long series of years, and to the almost total exclusion of notes, as the currency of all Lancashire, of the West Riding of Yorkshire, and a large portion of the other great manufacturing districts in the heart of England ". He added, " In those districts, we are told that bills were then to be had for all sums from five pounds to ten thousand, and at all dates not exceeding three months." [3]

In the absence of a system of banks with deposits transferable by cheques, the bill of exchange had manifold advantages. English banks at this period were small, private concerns and their notes circulated generally only within a limited area. But the bill, drawn, as it usually was, against commodities, had a wider field. It circulated because of the confidence each person had, not only in the person on whom it was drawn, but also in the person who had drawn it, and in the person from whom he had received it and whose endorsement it bore. It might very well appear, therefore, to be a safer document than the note of a country banker. Since it was payable only to a particular person and not to bearer there was little danger if it were lost. And, since it was payable at a date sometime ahead, its value increased with time : it bore interest to the holder. If, before the bill became due, the holder wanted cash he could discount the bill with a local banker, and the banker, in turn, if he wished, could rediscount with a London bank : it was an investment possessing a high degree of liquidity.

[1] Henry Thornton : *An Enquiry into the Nature and Effects of the Paper Credit of Great Britain* (1802). Reprint in McCulloch's *Scarce Tracts on Paper Currency and Banking* (1857), 164.

[2] Quoted by John Fullarton : *On the Regulation of Currencies* (second edition 1845), 33.

[3] Fullarton : *op. cit.*, 39.

These are reasons explaining the ubiquity of bills of exchange at this period. The special preference of Lancashire for bills rather than notes is a matter deserving of research. It arose, no doubt, out of a high degree of commercial confidence, no less than out of a low degree of trust in note-issuers, and the fact that Lancashire bought raw material from distant places and sold products in distant markets must also have engendered a preference for a document the circulation of which was not confined to the sphere of operations of a local bank. As time went on the domestic bill came to play a smaller part in commercial transactions : the increase of the stamp duties after the Napoleonic War dealt a blow to the system ; and the growth of large banks of deposits with many branches, together with the shortening of the customary terms of credit, led to a substitution of cheques for bills in inland trade during the later decades of the nineteenth century.[1] But in the period with which we are concerned cheques were in their infancy and the bill had no serious rival as a medium of exchange between traders.

When Peter Stubs had payments to make he might instruct his creditor to draw a bill on him. Below is an actual example.

£10   BELFAST 29th Octo: 1794
    Ten days after Sight pay Mr. Tho[s] Green or order ten pounds
Ster[l] value in Acco[t] which place to Acco[t] without further advice.
To M[r] Peter Stubs   from   THOS. LYLE.
      Warrington   Accepted
(97305)   P. STUBS Nov. 6th.

The bill bore an imprinted stamp of threepence. In this case Thomas Lyle was the drawer, Peter Stubs the drawee and Thomas Green the payee : after Stubs had written his name on the face of the bill he became the acceptor and was legally liable for payment. On the back of the bill was written " p. pro Thomas Green Thos. Ellison " : that is, the bill had been endorsed on behalf of Green. If now Green had chosen to send the bill to any other person to whom he was indebted that person would also have endorsed it : he in turn might have paid it away again, and so on. Inland bills drawn with a longer usance than the ten days of this one might sometimes bear a dozen or more endorsements. If, when the day of payment came, the acceptor failed to pay it the holder could take action not only against the drawer and the acceptor but also against all who had endorsed it ; and hence willingness to receive a bill in payment of a debt depended

---

[1] For the decline of the inland bill see W. T. C. King : *History of the London Discount Market*, 271–5.

on the confidence reposed in the intermediate endorsers, as well as in the other parties to the bill.

Generally bills were drawn only on persons of substance—though in July, 1805, there is reference to one drawn on a person who was only a workman. The more important of Stubs' customers were usually willing that he should draw on them : when in July, 1791, McLiran & Connachie of Glasgow, sent an order for files, they wrote, " If you be affraid of the Money you can draw in favour of any person here " ; and in December, 1793, Broom Price & Co. of Bristol wrote, " It will be more agreeable for you to draw on us for your account— at 2 mos. dated 1 January, 1794."

To avoid the trouble of drawing a bill and the expense of the stamp duty, many customers made payment to Stubs by bills which they had received from others ; and, correspondingly, when Stubs had payments to make, instead of asking his creditor to draw on him, he might remit bills which he had received. Just as the trader to-day keeps a balance at the bank on which he can draw cheques when necessary, so at this period a trader kept by him a supply of bills, and when a payment was required he would select from his stock such bills of the right maturity as would make up the sum due. In February, 1796, for example, a dealer, A. J. Sharp of Rugeley, who had delivered barley to Stubs, was asking for payment. At this time John Stubs, who was then sixteen years of age, had begun to assist his father in business ; and Peter wrote on Sharp's letter the following note to his son : " John, Examine the above and see the amount of the Bills we have sent him and get a Bill drawn with any we have by us to make up the balance. You will see by the Bill Book what will come in."

In remitting bills from his stock a trader would naturally select those payable in the neighbourhood in which his creditor resided or carried on business. In October, 1797, Chorley & Peet, knowing that Stubs had dealings in Sheffield, paid their debt to him by sending a bill drawn by one, P. Orr, on P. Cadman of Sheffield, payable at 21 days after sight. This bill Stubs sent to John Darwin of Sheffield, who placed it to his account for iron delivered to Stubs ; and on the expiration of the 21 days, Darwin, no doubt, presented it and obtained payment from Cadman. Similarly, in September, 1802, Stubs drew a bill for £80 on Auchie, Ure & Co. of Glasgow for files he had supplied to them : this he sent to David Mushet in payment for steel, leaving Mushet to collect from Auchie, Ure & Co. Again, in August, 1804, he drew on Hawksley & Sons of Sheffield, whom he had supplied with wire, and sent the bill to Walkers & Booth of Rotherham to set to his account for steel.

When a trader remitted a bill in this way it was, of course, necessary for him to endorse it, and if he omitted to do so the bill might be sent back to him. In acknowledging the receipt from Stubs of three bills in June, 1798, Walkers & Booth wrote, " As one of the bills has not your signature on the back and would be return'd with expenses if we sent it away, have taken the liberty of enclosing for your doing the needful." But that the methods of dealing with an omission of this sort were sometimes irregular is indicated by a letter of March, 1790, from Braithwaite & Backhouse of Kendal—a Quaker firm which might have been expected to be meticulous in such matters. Stubs had returned to them a bill they had sent him. Their reply was ". . . Sorry you should have the trouble of returning it for want of indorsement. Had you wrote Braithwaite & Backhouse no fault could have been found." Another irregularity of which traders were sometimes guilty was that of writing out a bill on paper without the official stamp : in June, 1805, W. Turner of Manchester returned to Stubs a bill, saying the person on whom it was drawn was a prisoner in the Fleet and adding, " It has hurt our credit, the banker not liking it on a/c of its being drawn without a stamp."

Evidently a trader might sometimes search through his stock in vain to find bills of the exact amount to pay a debt : in such case he would send the nearest equivalent and ask his creditor to hold over the difference, if a debit, or either set it to his account or remit, if a credit. When they sent Stubs a bill for £5 in March, 1790, J. & T. Barston of Grantham said they regretted they could not get one nearer the right amount ; and when in August, 1793, John Wilkinson of Leeds sent a bill for £17 15s. he added, " Nearest I had. Hope you will accept it in full for two parcels of files." Again, in January, 1793, when William Harrison of Chester sent a bill drawn by Thomas Brooke on Kerfoot Sons & Co. of Warrington, he asked Stubs to present it for payment and, when paid, to hand over to one Turner, an ironmonger of Warrington, the sum of £4, and put the remaining £6 to his account. It was not the practice to draw bills for sums less than £5, and even for amounts somewhat in excess of this it was often impossible to find bills : in February, 1805, a Belfast Quaker, Francis Bell, sent Stubs an English bank note for £5, saying he would have sent the balance, but found it difficult to get a bill for so small a sum.

Another feature of bills of exchange that might have been expected to give rise to difficulties was the varying dates at which they matured. One might think that the creditor would have taken bills only at their present value—at a discount varying with the period each had still to run. This was certainly the general practice at a later period ; [1] but in the seventeen-nineties it was only the larger merchants, and especially those trading in grain, who insisted on allowances for bills that had not reached maturity. John Port and George Stelfox, both of whom occasionally sold barley to Stubs, were meticulous in their claims to discount ; [2] but most of their fellows appear not to have troubled about it. In the steel, file and tool trades there is no evidence (as far as these records go) of any adjustment arising out of the usance of bills ; and that close calculation of discount was not a common practice among British industrialists at this period was explicitly stated by Henry Thornton in 1802 :

> The bill, when it is first drawn, is worth something less than a bank note, on account of its not being due until a distant day ; and the first receiver of it may be supposed to obtain a compensation for the inferiority of its value in the price of the article with which the bill is purchased . . .
>
> Bills, it is true, generally pass among traders in the country without there being any calculation or regular allowance of discount ; the reason of which circumstance is, that there is a generally understood period of time for which those bills may have to run, which, according to the custom of traders, are accepted as current payment. If any bill given in payment has a longer time than usual to run, he who received it is considered as so far favouring the person from whom he takes it ; and the favoured person has to compensate for this advantage, not, perhaps by a recompense of the same kind accurately calculated, but in the general adjustment of the pecuniary affairs of the two parties.

When a bill was presented for payment it might be met either by cash or by a draft on a banker payable within a few days' time, or even

[1] " My personal memory of trade only extends back to the year 1820," wrote a Manchester banker, William Langton, in 1877, " but at that time the Liverpool merchants received nothing but bills in payment from Manchester of their cotton invoices ; every such payment, if in what was called promiscuous paper, requiring a calculation of interest to make a settlement per appoint."—Ashton : *Economic and Social Investigations in Manchester, 1833–1933*, 85.

[2] In June, 1794, for instance, George Stelfox presented the following statement of claim to discount on bills :

	£	s.	s.	d.
50 Days upon	49	19	6	10
32 Days upon	10	–		10½
6 Days upon	36	19		5¼
34 Days upon	14	3	1	4
47 Days upon	18	–	2	3¼

	11	9

occasionally by a promissory note.[1]   In 1796 Stubs drew a bill on Jane
Green & Sons of Sheffield for £27 6s. and sent it in part payment
of his account to John Harrison & Son.   On 18 May, John Harrison
wrote to say he had presented the bill half a dozen times, but had always
been put off : first members of the firm had promised to meet it in
a few days, then they had objected that they had never authorized
Stubs to draw on them, and finally they had offered to pay in drafts at
two months.   Harrison told them it was not usual to take up bills
with drafts at two months when the bills had been due several weeks ;
and, after further disputation, the matter was finally settled by Green &
Sons sending to Stubs a short-date draft drawn by the Sheffield Bank
of Walker, Eyre & Stanley on the London bank of Down, Thornton &
Cornwall.

Requests to be allowed to postpone payment were fairly common :
if these were granted it meant the cancellation of existing bills and the
drawing of others maturing at a later date.   The same thing happened
in effect, when a person on whom a bill had been drawn was allowed
to pay it, not in cash or by a bank draft, but by a bill on another trader
payable at some time ahead.   In April, 1793, Joseph Tarratt of Wolverhampton sent Stubs a bill on J. Holland, ironmonger of Warrington,
payable at fourteen days.   Cash was hard to come by at that time
and Tarratt therefore added, " If he should offer to take it up with a
good bill don't refuse it."   Among the Sheffield factors who bought
files and wire of Stubs in his later years was the firm of Hawksley &
Sons.   Towards the end of 1803 Stubs drew a bill on them for £150,
payable 40 days after sight, and informed them that he had done so.
They replied that " money at this time is uncommonly scarce ", and,
therefore, instead of accepting his bill, they sent another drawn by
them on Ransom, Morland & Co. at 60 days.   Other instances of the
same kind can be cited from the correspondence with the concern of
R. Price & Co. of Bristol.   When, in July, 1804, a bill drawn on them
was presented to their bank for payment it was found that the banker's
clerk had been instructed to hold it up.   The firm was unable to get
funds owing to the failure of other businesses ; and they therefore asked
Stubs to draw again at two months and charge them for the stamp and
interest.   Again, in December, 1805, Price & Co. wrote to say they
could not pay before Christmas a bill Stubs had drawn on them, since
a large payment they had expected from Canada had failed to reach
them.   Once more they asked Stubs to re-draw on them at two months.

[1] In sending a promissory note in February, 1802, Z. Rowton of
Northampton wrote, " You may depend on my note being as duly
hon[d] as those of the Bank of England."

A request for postponement of payment was often the herald of actual default. There is evidence that bills often (perhaps normally) circulated before they had obtained acceptance. In October, 1805, R. Greaves of Manchester wrote, " Yours informing me the draft had not been accepted. You may either send the draft to yr. Banker or negotiate it yourself, for you may depend upon it that the draft will be honourably paid." If, however, there was any fear that the persons on whom a bill was drawn might default, it was of some importance to ensure that it should be accepted, so that legal action could be taken in the last resort. In the case of Holland, mentioned above, Joseph Tarratt drew another bill in the autumn of 1793 and sent it to Stubs to collect. When Stubs called he found that Holland was away from home and he therefore sent the bill back to Wolverhampton. In reply, Tarratt said he was sorry Stubs had not kept it until Holland's return, when he might have obtained its acceptance. As it was clear that Holland was likely to fail—he actually became bankrupt a month later —it was highly desirable that his creditors should have legal proof of their claims.

Just as Stubs helped Tarratt in his troubles with Holland, so Tarratt helped Stubs in his efforts to obtain payment from the firm of Grosvenor & Perry of Wolverhampton, who had failed to meet a bill due to Stubs in the summer of 1797. Stubs sent the returned bill to Tarratt, asking him to present it for payment a second time. On his doing so John Grosvenor promised to take it up the following day, but failed to keep his word, and again promised to remit in the morning. Tarratt, however, was sceptical : " I have my doubts about it for his paper has been coming back for some time." Stubs, therefore, took legal proceedings. On 23 September William Perry, Grosvenor's partner wrote : " To our utter astonishment we had a letter from your attorney, J. Nicholson . . . saying you had arrested J. Grosvenor. You should have informed us the moment it came back—particularly before you went to violence. We were upon a journey or you would have heard from us before." On 11 November Grosvenor finally settled his account by sending Stubs a draft for £105 10s. 3d. on Gibbon & Co. with an assurance that he was not a man of straw and that " the badness of the times alone has been the cause of this business ".[1]

[1] Another instance of failure to meet a bill occurred in 1800. In February of that year Spencer & Greave of Skipton wrote to say they were surprised to find that their draft on a certain Gledhill had not been paid. They asked Peter Stubs to present it again and " if he does not pay it he may be induced to accept it and promise to pay in a week's time. Then we can give it to an attorney if necessary."

When a bill with names endorsed on it was refused acceptance or payment the holder had a claim on the endorsers. In October, 1805, John Andrew & Co. of Kilmarnock wrote concerning such a bill which they had endorsed and sent to Stubs. They said that it had been sent to them by Bryden & Blackstock, umbrella-makers of Manchester, whose name was on the back of the bill above theirs ; and instead of themselves making payment to Stubs they asked him to make application to these prior endorsers. As careful Scots, they added, " If possible keep off our postage, likewise 1s., and you can account to us for it again." In such cases of refusal to pay, it was incumbent on the holder of the bill to send it back to the last endorser immediately ; for if there were any delay he might forfeit his claim. On 22 April, 1805, Stubs returned to Samuel King of Hull a draft for £20 which he had received from King, but which had been dishonoured. King acknowledged the return of the bill and added, " I have wrote to both Drakenfeld & Co. and John Heelis the two former indorsers : am apprehensive they will think themselves exonerated from taking the Bill as it has somewhere met with a considerable delay and on that account the men of law here are of opinion that the indorsers are discharged. Should it turn out so the consequence will be that you will have the bill back." Ten days later, on 4 May, King informed Stubs that the drawee of the bill was a prisoner in York Castle and that it was therefore impossible to get the bill taken up by him. The fact that it had been retained twenty days beyond the time at which an unpaid bill should have been returned had led the first endorser to refuse it for a considerable time. He had evidently, however, been persuaded to give way, and King therefore sent Stubs a new bill for £20 in place of the one that had been dishonoured.

When a bill was refused acceptance or payment the holder might take it to a notary, who would present it again, and ' note ' it : that is, he would attach to the bill a piece of paper giving the reason for the refusal to accept or pay. For certain purposes it might be necessary to go a step further and have the bill ' protested ' : that is to have drawn up a legal document protesting against the drawers and endorsers for loss and damage.[1] The charges for these processes had to be met by the parties responsible for the bill. In 1793 Samuel Timmins of

---

[1] " If an action be brought upon a bill which has been only noted, it will be necessary to produce a witness in court, to prove that the bill was duly and properly presented for payment : but if the bill has been protested, the production of the protest will be sufficient evidence." —J. W. Gilbart : *History, Principles and Practice of Banking* (ed. Ernest Sykes, 1907), Vol. I, 175.

Birmingham sent Stubs a bill for £80 drawn on a certain Dawson, and when the time for payment arrived Dawson was unable to meet it in cash. Stubs evidently, therefore, sent it to a notary, and on 9 April Timmins wrote, " I yesterday received back Wm. Dawson's acceptance value £33 with the enormous charge of 11/10$^{s\ d}$ cover'd with a stamped sheet from the notary publick, which to me seems a new plan of returning Bills . . . (Noting and protesting I think very proper)." He also said he had given Richardson for the returned bill a draft on Taylor & Lloyd at seven days' sight.

When Stubs drew bills on customers in order to make payment to others he was not always scrupulous to ensure that he was in credit to the full amount of the draft. As has been seen, it was his practice to keep running accounts, balanced only at intervals of twelve months or longer, with his regular customers. It is probable that, with the loose accounting methods of his day, he was not always aware of the existing state of his balance with particular firms, and so he might fall into errors of this kind unwittingly. Illustration can be found in his dealings with Hawksley & Sons, to whom reference has been made above. In August, 1804, Stubs drew on this concern for £150 at 2 months and sent the bill to Walkers & Booth of Rotherham in payment for steel. His letter informing Hawksley & Sons that he had drawn on them brought the following sharp reply :

We are much surprised to see that you should have drawn for £74 more than the wire amounts to : we suppose by acting thus you imagine that we are made of money : we are assured you must know that we can obtain no remittances from the Continent owing to the high exchange on London. Moreover you are not allowing the usual Credit for a running Acc^t of 12 Ms. We shall honour your draft this time, but have a care for the future in drawing before the time.

When a bill was to be drawn on a customer it was a point of courtesy to notify him at once.[1] " Whenever you draw on me I expect to have advice given the same day," wrote J. J. Bing of London in December, 1795, " as it is a rule with me neither to accept nor pay a bill unless advis'd thereof. I don't value the expense of postage." Here again Stubs occasionally slipped. On 12 October, 1805, James Dowell of Bristol protested that he had only just received advice that Stubs had drawn on him for £40. " I have a right to be consulted ", he said. " How am I to know what obligations are existing or how to provide for such uncertainty. You must remit me for this draft before it is

[1] Some customers required long notice : in March, 1795, Thomas Jackson of London asked for two months' notice of any bill Stubs might have the right to draw on him.

due, if you draw again for the same amount." A week later, on 19 October, he repeated that he must always have notice of intention to draw on him : Stubs, he insisted, must either send him a draft on London at 2 months, rather before the bill on Dowell was to fall due, or alter the original bill to 3 months : otherwise he would not accept. Stubs was willing to alter the tenor of the bill to 3 months, but now wished to have it payable in London instead of in Bristol. To this Dowell gave grudging assent, but added, " By requiring me to accept yr. draft at 3 mos. in London I am placed in ye same predicament as if you drew at 2 mos. in Bristol, since I must give my Bankers notice 30 days previous to it becoming due. I have altered ye date to ye 29th which will form a partial recompense." In the letter of 19 October, Dowell expressed surprise that Stubs should want to have the bill paid in London. " You need not be at so great trouble to negotiate a bill on Bristol when Castle & Co. receive thousands in ye year from yr. town. Their customers I presume wd. gladly give you silver and copper for such Bills : they do so at Birmingham and Liverpool and it ought to be so at yr. town." [1]

It should be clear that many, if not all, of the difficulties that arose from a bill currency created by traders drawing on other traders could be obviated by an efficient banking system. The chief function of the country bank of the eighteenth century—apart from the issue of notes —was to act as an intermediary in bills of exchange. Instead of keeping his own portfolio of bills, a trader could send those he received direct to his banker, who would discount them for him and set the amount to his credit. Instead of himself taking or sending a bill for acceptance or payment, he could leave this troublesome business to a banker.[2] Instead of seeking for bills of the nearest equivalent to the payment he had to make, he could draw on his banker for the exact amount and date. And, to go a step further, instead of drawing on his banker, a trader could get his banker to give him a bill drawn by the banker on a London correspondent : it was by means of such bankers' drafts on London that a large part of the business of the country was transacted at this period. To give only a few of many instances that might be cited : the firm of J. & G. Lewis paid Stubs by drafts of the

[1] Stubs himself had dealings with Robert Castle & Co. of Bristol, who supplied the *White Bear* with gin.

[2] On 15 October, 1805, I. T. Miller wrote : " On my coming to Town yesterday I recd. a Letter from you respecting a Bill drawn by you, which will be paid when due. My son informs me the Person who brought the Bill said it was a great way to come again after the Bill. I always found the Banker had the Bills left for acceptance which he ought to have done."

Birmingham bank of Spooner, Attwood & Co. on Sir John Esdaile & Son of London ; Jane Green & Sons by drafts of Walker, Eyre & Stanley of Sheffield on Down, Thornton & Cornwall of London ; G. & I. Shaw and J. Reynolds, by drafts of Beckett, Calverley & Co. of Leeds on Baron Dimsdale & Co. of London ; and Braithwaite & Backhouse by drafts of John Wakefield Sons & Co. of Kendal on Masterman & Co. of London. Beside supplying drafts which would find a more ready circulation than those drawn by traders, the private bankers would sometimes guarantee trade bills drawn or endorsed by their clients. When in June, 1805, Stubs had to send back for non-payment a bill received from them, A. & R. Watson of Glasgow replaced it by a draft on Glynn & Co., the well-known London house, and said, " In future should any bills with our Indorsation be refused, upon applying to our friends Sir Rb. Glynn & Co. they will retire them for our honour." [1]

In the foregoing pages reference has been made to two Warrington concerns which acted as intermediaries in effecting payments for clients in other towns : one of these was Thomas Lyon & Co., the other Walter Kerfoot, Sons & Co., solicitors. Some time in the early 'eighties Lyon and Kerfoot had joined with a sugar-boiler, Joseph Parr, to set up the Warrington Bank, then known as Parr, Lyon & Co. (and later simply as Parr's) which is now merged in the West-minster Bank. Peter Stubs kept an account with Parr, Lyon & Co. When he needed ready money for the payment of wages and so on he could obtain it by discounting bills with them ; and when he had commercial payments to make, for which his own supply of bills was inappropriate, he could obtain from them drafts on their London agent, Crofts, Devaynes, Dawes & Noble.[2] Moreover, for payments which had to be made locally he was able to draw cheques. Mention of cheques on Parr, Lyon & Co. is made in letters or invoices from a number of men who provided Stubs with materials, as for example, M. Jameson, who supplied coal in 1794, and James Robinson, who supplied barley in 1798. Cheques, however, had not yet come into common use among traders, and it would appear that most of those drawn by Stubs were payable to people in the immediate neigh-bourhood of Warrington, or in Manchester or Liverpool.

The account was opened on 6 October, 1791. The pass books [3]

---

[1] In technical language Glynn & Co. were the " case of need ".

[2] For the history of Parr's Bank see T. E. Gregory : *The Westminster Bank*, II, 24 ff.

[3] Stubs had to provide his own bank books. He bought them of John Hadock, printer, of Warrington, at 4s. each.

show that Stubs was debited for bills and cash supplied to him, as well as for miscellaneous payments made by the bank on his behalf for stamps, occasional lottery tickets and excise duties. On all these debits commission was charged each half-year at the rate of $\frac{1}{4}$ of 1 per cent.[1] On the other hand, Stubs was credited for cash and bills paid in. Sometimes he received interest from the bank, at other times he paid interest; the fact that he was charged interest in the half-year January–June, 1792, when his deposits far exceeded his withdrawals (and when, both at the beginning and at the end of the period, he had a credit balance), suggests that the bills he sent to the bank were credited at their value on maturity and that the interest charged represented discount on these. If it had been the practice of Stubs to use the bank as a modern business man uses his, the pass books would give a fairly true statement of turnover. There is ample evidence, however, that only a part of his receipts went into the bank and only a part of his payments was made by bills or cash supplied by it. Money received at the inn would, no doubt, be used for wages, household expenses and minor purchases; and bills received from customers were often endorsed and passed on to those to whom Stubs was indebted, without going through the bank. (For example, a payment of £333 10s. made to Walkers & Booth by eight separate bills on 17 January, 1800, is reflected in the pass book by only a single draft for £126 12s. : the other seven bills came from the stock which Stubs held outside the bank.) The figures on the opposite page must, therefore, be taken as representing not the total volume of transactions, but only that (perhaps smaller) portion which passed through the hands of Parr, Lyon & Co. The figures in the last column represent the balance at the end of each half-year, 30 June or 31 December—indicated respectively by (1) and (2). The minus sign denotes interest charged by the bank or debit balance.

The volume of payments into the bank, it will be noticed, was always greater in the first half of the year than in the second. This was due to the fact that the larger customers had twelve-months' running accounts : they made up their books on 31 December and remitted the amounts due in the early months of the following year. Generally, but not invariably, the same was true of payments out of the bank, for Stubs also tended to pay his debts after the end of the year ; but since he drew cash to pay wages, as well as bills to pay commercial debts, when industrial activity was increasing his withdrawals from the bank were sometimes larger in the second half of

---

[1] A commission of $\frac{1}{4}$ of 1 per cent. was the rule in Manchester in 1832. See Gregory, op. cit., I, 29.

	Debits. £ s. d.	Credits. £ s. d.	Commission. £ s. d.	Interest. £ s. d.	Balance. £ s. d.
1791 (2)	292 13 7	291 15 0	1 14 5	+ 1 13 0	+ 3 11 5
1792 (1)	303 1 1	785 9 5	15 2	− 13 9	+ 484 10 10
1792 (2)	583 11 5	295 19 6	1 9 2	+ 12 1 9	+ 207 11 6
1793 (1)	1,057 6 3	901 6 9	2 12 10	+ 1 12 3	+ 50 11 5
1793 (2)	421 18 1	376 2 0	1 1 1	− 8 0 9	+ 2 19 4
1794 (1)	723 8 1	700 5 10	1 16 2	+ 2 0 10	− 14 9 7
1795 (1)	422 17 7	663 10 6	1 1 2	+ 4 2 7	+ 228 16 7
1795 (2)	684 17 5	669 0 0	1 14 3	+ 5 11 7	+ 216 6 10
1796 (1)	487 1 5	615 13 6	1 4 4	+ 8 14 8	+ 343 14 7
1796 (2)	822 11 10	712 17 11	2 1 1	+ 7 6 1	+ 239 14 1
1797 (1)	412 1 10	562 17 6	2 10 0	+ 7 18 3	+ 395 19 5
1797 (2)	1,004 19 9	771 6 0	2 10 3	+ 9 16 10	+ 167 1 0
1798 (1)	860 11 5	758 0 4	2 3 0	+ 12 16 7	+ 72 4 5
1798 (2)	915 14 0	1,227 2 3	2 5 9	+ 11 8 8	+ 392 17 7
1799 (1)	927 0 10	613 14 10	2 6 4	+ 4 1 8	+ 88 13 4
1799 (2)	1,167 7 2	1,223 7 6	2 18 4	+ 8 3 3	+ 145 2 9
1800 (1)	635 12 11	808 6 1	1 11 9	+ 15 13 7	+ 323 16 9
1800 (2)	959 8 2	1,302 10 6	2 7 11	+ 15 16 9	+ 679 5 7
1801 (1)	1,735 5 0	811 9 5	4 6 9	+ 15 16 9	− 235 9 7
	519 17 7	846 14 3	1 5 11	+ 4 1 4	+ 94 5 6
1804 (1)	4,059 8 11	2,779 5 1	10 3 0	− 30 7 5	− 579 2 0
1805 (1)	3,574 8 4	3,903 9 7	8 18 8	− 52 15 4	− 1,902 13 11
1805 (2)	3,273 8 8	2,979 17 3	8 8 0	− 60 11 7	− 1,638 1 7
1806 (1)	2,881 14 10	4,403 3 3	7 4 0	− 48 3 11	− 2,002 8 5
1806 (2)	2,696 2 0	2,164 10 10	6 14 10	− 27 2 9	− 538 7 5
					− 1,106 0 11

the year. Another point worthy of notice is the increase of debits (and to a less extent of credits) in times of financial stress, such as the first half of 1793 and 1797 and the second half of 1800. At such times creditors would naturally prefer to be paid in bank paper instead of in bills drawn on other traders without the endorsement of a banker. It is unfortunate that the pass book for the years between 1 July, 1801, and 1 July, 1804, is missing, for it was during this period that the relation between banker and client underwent a change. Up to 1801 Stubs had normally maintained a credit balance and received interest from the bank ; by 1804 he had become an habitual borrower, paying interest to the bank. In the earlier years he had used the bank primarily as a repository for his cash balances and as a supplier of means of remittance : in the later years he had come to adopt the modern practice of relying on bank loans for part of his trading capital. The change of attitude apparently came just at the time of transition from domestic to factory or workshop production. Stubs, it would appear, built up his business with his own resources (aided to a slight extent by credit from those who supplied the raw material). When —but only when—he was sufficiently well-established to invest in buildings and equipment and to produce in a large way did the bank begin to provide capital on a significant scale. Was this, one wonders, the experience of other industrialists also ? Did the country banks have little to do with the inception of businesses but much to do with their subsequent expansion ? We are shamefully ignorant of such matters, and it would be well if some student would make the part played by the banking system in the financing of the Industrial Revolution the subject of specialized research.

III

In the last decade of the eighteenth century the course of English industry was far from smooth. The period was punctuated by recurrent crises in each of which the normal circulation of bills, described above, broke down or, at least, worked only imperfectly. No attempt will be made to describe in detail the causes of these interruptions to the flow of credit : the purpose of this section is simply to illustrate, from letters received by Stubs, the difficulties of making and receiving payments at such times.

When war between France and England broke out in February, 1793, there was a sudden collapse of credit. For some years past there had been taking place an expansion of both the number of country banks and the volume of their note issues ; and during the later months of 1792 nervous clients had shown a tendency to bring back their notes and withdraw cash from the country banks. Following the usual procedure, the country banks had applied to their London agents, and these, in turn, had withdrawn gold from the Bank of England. Even before France declared war, then, there was a demand for liquidity. The outbreak of hostilities brought a run on banks in all parts of the country, and the failure of large numbers of these created a gap in the circulation for which the issue of Exchequer Bills by the Government was only a partial solution. In these circumstances traders looked askance at bills and bankers' drafts which normally would have been taken without question ; and everywhere there was a demand for coin. Many well-conducted businesses found it impossible to meet their debts in forms of payment acceptable to their creditors : the number of commercial and financial bankruptcies rose, according to Silberling's figures, from 638 in 1792 to 1,377 in 1793.

Those with money owing from Peter Stubs were urgent in their requests for payment. On 28 March Stephen Barber of Walsall sent a bill to Caldwell & Whitley, asking them to collect it from Stubs and send the coin received by Morris' first waggon, " as we are so circumstanced in this country we have not cash to go on with ". It is possible, however, that in spite of such incidents Stubs at first underestimated the seriousness of the crisis. For on Monday, 8 April, he called at the counting-house of Bold, Richard & Conway in Liverpool, gave an order for 500 bushels of barley, and (in consideration of a reduction in price from 5s. 3d. to 5s.) promised to pay in guineas. A letter was sent to him the same day confirming the oral contract. On his return home, however, Stubs evidently discovered that he had been over-sanguine in his expectation of obtaining guineas, and he, therefore, wrote countermanding the order. The result was the following letter from the Liverpool merchants, dated 11 April :

We are a little surprised at the receipt of your two Letters of the 9th and 10th Inst. However as we have never yet suffered ourselves to be imposed upon or treated unhandsomely, we are resolved not to suffer it in this instance. Annexed you have the Affidavit of Mr. Bolton who you spoke to on this Business ; and if you do not think proper after this proof to receive the Barley and have the guineas in readiness *early on Saturday Morng.* (when our J. Conway proposes being in Warrington) we shall put the Business in Mr. Kerfoot's hands to settle for us.

The annexed statement was to the effect that Charles Bolton had appeared before Henry Blundell, Esq., a Justice of the Peace for Liverpool, and had made oath on the Holy Evangelists that Stubs had promised to take the barley and pay guineas down. Whether the guineas were forthcoming or not is uncertain ; but the barley was delivered and paid for in some form or other. It turned out to be of poor quality ; and on 27 May, Bold, Richard & Conway, in a very different temper, asked Stubs to say what allowance he thought reasonable as compensation.

The crisis involved more, however, than a dearth of actual cash. Traders and bankers were reluctant to allow customers to draw on them, and the bill circulation itself shrank. As already mentioned, a large part of the trade of the provinces was carried on by bills drawn on London houses, for these normally had a wider currency than those drawn on local traders or country bankers. In ordinary times such bills would pass from one trader to another before acceptance ; but in the circumstances of 1793 it was a matter of elementary prudence to ensure that bills would be met. When, on 10 June, James Newton of Newark sent Stubs a draft of his local bank on a London house he wrote, " Tis best plan now-a-days to send Bills and drafts quick up to London for acceptance—tho' I believe our present Bank is strong as any in the Kingdom." If the practice became common it must have intensified the shortage of means of remittance in the provinces.

Of this shortage there is ample evidence in the correspondence. On 29 March John Unsworth of Manchester wrote to say he could not pay his debt but would do so " as soon as things get right ". More than two months later the account was still unpaid, and a letter of 9 June from Richard Shaw, who had visited Unsworth on behalf of Stubs, suggests that the general situation in Manchester was deteriorating : " Things here seem to bear a much wors app. than they did when I wass here Last say a fortnight since and I doubt the storm is far from being blown over." About the same time, John Astley of Blackburn wrote to say, " I cannot possibly remit you a bill for that ret'd, owing to the very awkward situation our Trade in this Town is at present " ; and in the same month William Harris of Ashton, writing from Hull, said, " I get orders plenty but Money very bad to come at." From Newcastle came word that the affairs of Nicholas Teesdale were in a bad way and that he was unable to pay a sum of 10 guineas owed to Stubs. As has been seen, Samuel Timmins of Birmingham found himself in difficulties ; and, in May, James Dowell of Bristol (in a letter complaining that goods ordered two months earlier had not been delivered) said, " If you suppose that ye Colour of ye Times be sufficient to justify your Intention to withhold Goods I by no means object to ye determination."

The larger wholesalers with whom Stubs had dealings were especially hard hit. As early as 9 February, Warham, Potts & Smith of Leeds wrote to say that a request for a bill had come at a time when they were much straitened. On 1 May they made a small remittance of £15, saying they had waited in vain for other bills to come in, and that they had had one for £1,400 returned, unpaid, from Scotland. Nearly three months later Thomas Warham, who was on a journey, sent a mere £40 from Manchester : he added that he would be in Warrington in a few days but feared he would have nothing more for Stubs, and that he had sent this bill beforehand for fear it should be taken from him at Ashton. On 17 September one of his partners wrote to say they regretted they were unable to make a remittance : Mr. Warham was in Scotland and they were expecting something from him by every post : " We never war so put about for Money."

Scotland, it would appear, was one of the last places in which to hope to secure means of payment. On 2 May, Archibald Turner of Glasgow wrote, " The machine makers here are mostly brook and I have lost considerable with them all." ; and on the same day another Glasgow trader, James Auchie, cancelled an order, " affairs in this place being in a very confused way ". In a later letter of 11 May Auchie gave further details of the situation he was in : " . . . no settlement can be got either by Bills or Cash, which of course the Bills on the Circle drains us of our cash and these we must prepare for, and as we lay in five-sixths parts of our goods and more at money prices we must endeavour to keep as few in hand as possible at this time ". In September another Glasgow merchant, William Johnstone wrote to say that the condition of Scotland was deplorable and that he was unable to make a remittance ; and, as late as February, 1794, he asserted that " the general stagnation of things in this country . . . makes it impossible for us to perform regular payments ". By this time, however, the panic was over : on 16 April, Archibald Turner told Stubs he believed Johnstone was in a position to pay, and he offered, if Stubs decided to prosecute, to look after the matter.

During the following four years trade improved and remittances resumed their ordinary course. In September, 1794, the son of John Bacon, a Macclesfield cutler, wrote to say that his father " from pressing and political circumstances has been under the painful necessity of leaving the country "—an event which, it is just possible, was connected with the prosecution of the Corresponding Societies in that year. Stubs' share in the stock of Bacon's shop came to £1 7s. 9d. But instances of failure to pay are very rare at this time ; and letters from customers in 1796 give indications of boom condi-

I

tions. In February, John Harrison & Son of Sheffield wrote, " We have some large orders for ye American trade in Sheffield. Ours is more country trade as I suppose yours. That also is improving." In March John Parkin reported that all the tilts were full of steel. In a letter asking for work, Jonathan Cranage said he heard Stubs was very busy ; and John Appleton wrote from Liverpool to say, " Business has been so brisk with Mr. Green that I have almost been pulled out of the shop by him for work . . . everybody is so busy that I can get no assistance." The demand for files was very keen and prices were raised.

In 1796 the Bank of England suffered a drain of gold to France, which was in process of returning to the gold standard after the disastrous experiment with the assignats ; and although a restriction of discounts in London caused specie once more to flow into England, the needs of trade, and some anxiety as to the state of credit, led to a withdrawal of guineas into circulation. To what extent the situation abroad, or to what extent Government borrowing from the Bank at home, was responsible for the precarious position at the beginning of 1797 need not be discussed here. Suffice it to say that the landing of the French convicts in Pembrokeshire on 25 February, precipitated the crisis that led to the suspension of cash payments on the following day. Even before this, a number of banks had closed, and, as in 1793, there was a shortage of means of payment. This time, however, the issue of small notes by the Bank of England, as well as by the country banks, relieved the demand for cash ; and though bankruptcies increased somewhat (from 749 in 1796 to 871 in 1797) [1] there was no such widespread failure of businesses as in the previous crisis. That there was some difficulty in getting payment, however, may be illustrated by a letter of 12 May from John Whitley (of Clowes & Whitley) who was on a visit to London : it concerned a draft that had not been paid :

You will readily conceive the shuffles of litigious people which is the case here. I never think of negociating a D'ft on a customer except I expect him to be as regular as a Banker—such I have generally found S. & B. . . . Such is the scarcity of moneys here that the first houses are glad to make any shuffling excuse rather than pay their debts. I think truly things wear a more gloomy appearance here than they do in the country . . . the people here seem ripe for anything.

If the shortage of guineas was overcome by the issue of the £1 and £2 notes of the Bank there remained the problem of small change. As the prices of silver and copper had been rising for some time,

[1] Silberling, *loc. cit.*

coins had been melted down ; and employers were hard put to it to obtain cash for the payment of wages. To some extent the difficulty had been met by private enterprise : token coins had been manufactured by industrialists, and some of these came to have a widespread circulation. The issue by the Government of the Spanish dollars in March, and the stamping of copper twopences and pennies by Matthew Boulton, under Government contract, in July, did something to meet the situation ; and in some areas the traders' tokens ceased to circulate. In September, 1797, John Sherwin of Burslem wrote to Stubs saying, " I should be glad to send you some Macclesfield and Anglesey halfpence if they pass with you because they are stopt with us." But whether or not the offer was accepted is not known.[1]

It would appear from the correspondence of Stubs that actual political events and the rumours to which they gave rise were more disturbing to trade at this time than any defect in the monetary system. Foreign trade was impeded by war, and domestic trade reacted to foreign. " I am sorry to inform you that the files you sent me is now laying at Hull ", wrote James Cam of Sheffield on 9 February, 1797, " and my Skipper informs me that all English Goods his prohibited into Sweden." " The number of ships that are every week taken belonging here has affected everyone . . ." said Thomas Kirkup of Sunderland in a letter of July 5, " Business is nearly at a standstill but it is to be hoped the blessing of peace is not far off." Unfortunately for Thomas Kirkup it was very far off ; and in little over twelve months he was a bankrupt. " I hope you will not hesitate in sending up the undermentioned order not with standing the prevailing talk of the French invading England ", wrote James Sibbald of Manchester on March 10 : he, too, was to go bankrupt before the first phase of the war with the French was brought to an end.

If the crisis of 1797 was less acute than its predecessor its effects were long-drawn-out. As late as February, 1798, Warham, Potts & Smith were still finding difficulty in making remittances. " Truly sorry we can't assist you at this time ", they wrote. " We have so many '95 and '96 accounts *unsettled*, it keeps us constantly on the

[1] The Macclesfield tokens were issued by Charles Roe, founder of the Macclesfield copper works and lessee of the Coniston mines, 1758–95. A token with the head of Charles Roe on the obverse is in the Ruskin Museum, Coniston. The Anglesey coinage was issued by Thomas Williams, senior partner in the Paris and Mona copper-mining companies, Anglesey, as well as in others elsewhere. For Williams see H. Hamilton : *The English Brass and Copper Industries, passim.*

stretch for money." Slowly trade improved. But in 1799 a recession occurred—the result partly of harvest failure at home [1] and partly of the financial crisis in Hamburg. Once again, there was pressure and a shortage of the means of remittance. On 1 August Reginald Owen of Croft wrote to say that Lewis of Birmingham was pressing him for payment. " No one wishes to pay my credit better than I do. I had speculated and built so far for my circumstances, the War comeing on or I could with Gods blessing have cleared my self. . . . I have begun to brew my own beer—I never expected Mr. Pens to have come upon me as he did without ever asking me to settle and had good security on a Second Mortgage—I buy my Malt from him." Stubs himself had to forgo payments. In sending a draft for £9, on 3 May, W. Hutchinson of Wakefield wrote, " I should have sent you a Bill in a month if your son had not behaved in so Genteel a manner —times is so bad we must bear a little with one another." And in a letter of 7 November Thomas Warham of Leeds observed, " I find our account is getting backwards again and had intended sending you 70 or 80 £. But an unlucky bill for £400 found its way back to us about 10 days ago."

Difficulties of making remittances continued into the year 1800. " There never was such a cry out for Money at Liverpool as at the present time ", remarked George Lewis of Birmingham on 1 February ; and on the same day Spencer & Greave of Skipton wrote regretting that their draft on Gledhill had not been met.[2] Until the coming of peace in October, 1801, indeed, conditions of stringency seem to have prevailed. On 14 January, 1801, Reginald Owen of Croft wrote, " Never where things in a more distressed state than at present. All work to live. And could not if we all did not work as hard as Possible." And that this was not merely a case of local depression is proved by other letters—as, for example, by one from William Harris of Ashton in which he says, " My son is out. In all his letters he complains hevily he cannot get payd."

Business men are notoriously more vocal about their distresses than about their good fortune. If one were to take at its face value every statement concerning the slackness of trade and shortage of money, it would be possible to argue that depression was endemic and not

---

[1] The failure of the harvest led to corn riots, for which see Ashton and Sykes : *The Coal Industry of the Eighteenth Century*, 129. On 30 May, 1799, William Wilbey of Wakefield wrote : " Sorry I was not at home when Mr. Stubs was here, but was a Soldier on that day, being a small Riot on the high price of Corn, but no Mischief done."

[2] *Supra*, 109 n.

merely periodic. The accumulation of evidence for the years 1793, 1797, and 1799–1800 is, however, such as cannot be ignored. From the opening of the new century to the end of the period with which we are concerned individual complaints were frequent ; failures to obtain remittances from abroad led to failures to make payment at home ; and the oscillation from war to peace and peace to war brought loss and bankruptcy to particular concerns.[1] But there was no such general collapse of credit as in the periods here considered. To continue the recital of passages from letters of customers referring to individual, as distinct from communal misfortune, would add nothing of significance to the substance of this chapter.

[1] The following examples will suffice. In March, 1802, John Crompton of London wrote, " I was in hopes before this to have received some orders in your line, but the uncertainty which has and still prevails respecting Peace, has induced the Merchts. abroad to suspend giving their orders." In August of the same year a Thomas Allen sent news of the failure of an old customer of Stubs : " I am extremely sorry to inform you that Mr. James Rawlins of Red Lion Street is under the painful necessity of calling a meeting of his Creditors . . . at the Baptist's Head Coffee House, Aldermansbury. . . . Mr. Rawlins for some time has been embarked in a Trade to Jamaica, under the immediate inspection of his Son and Partner. . . . But from the sudden Cessation of Hostilities producing a great alteration in the Markets, the remittances have not been equal to the demands which Mr. Rawlins had to meet ; however he did flatter himself that he should eventually be able to satisfy all the demands of his Creditors, but from the melancholy intelligence of the death of his son in Jamaica (being in the hands of Strangers) he now finds it absolutely necessary to consult his creditors." On 12 June, 1805, M. Laverack of Hull wrote, " I am sorry I have it not in my power at present to comply with your request. I can assure you that I want upwards of 400 £ of my last's year's Accounts and cannot tell how long I may yet be out of it. However I expect in the course of a month, we shall have some of the Baltic Ships of whom I want considerable sums for Goods sent this Spring and you may depend upon having a Remittance at that time with an order." On 3 November, 1805, J. J. Bing of London wrote, " Your draft 2 Mo. for £30 has not appeared but comes due at a very awkward time of Year, and the present embarrassed state of matters on the Continent stops all Commerce and Remittance as you must naturally Indulge, if you would withdraw said Draft and make the same become due in February will be much oblig'd to you."

CHAPTER NINE

THE FILE-MAKER AND HIS FAMILY

I

THE relations of the manufacturer and innkeeper with workers, merchants, customers, carriers and bankers have now been surveyed : it remains only to say something of Stubs himself and of those nearest to him. At the present day a man's business is normally a thing apart from his personal and domestic life : in the eighteenth century the two were intimately related. It is the good fortune of the biographer that this should have been so ; for it means that the instinct which led to the preservation of almost every business record has saved from destruction many letters and other documents that throw light on the character of Peter Stubs, as well as on the social circle in which his life was set.

If the typical industrialist of this period was (as is sometimes suggested) an austere nonconformist, penurious in his ways, and looking with distaste on the pleasures of his fellows, Stubs was far removed from type. He adhered to the Church of England, had his children baptized, and paid the rent for his pew with regularity. He was strongly patriotic. Soon after the outbreak of the war with France, in 1793, he changed the newspaper he bought of the bookseller, William Eyres, from the neutral *General Evening Post* to the more actively ministerialist *Sun*. When, in 1798, a body of volunteers, the " Bluebacks " was raised in Warrington, his son John became a private in the third company—and so, perhaps, saw such active service as was involved in the suppression of a riot of Irishmen in Bridge Street in 1799. And when, on the resumption of hostilities in 1803, the volunteers were revived under the name of " Robin Redbreasts ", Peter Stubs made a donation to their funds, and John became a lieutenant in the corps.[1]

[1] One John Baker of Liverpool wrote offering him an officer's cap for £1 3s. : it had a piece of leather behind " to let down when it rains to keep the water from the neck ". He offered also a leather cockade and " pretty good Feathers made from Geese from 1/6 to 2/6 ea. all green for the Light Comp^y, all white for the Grenadeers and red and white for the Batalion Comp^{ys} ". For reference to the riot and other

Like every other innkeeper of his day Stubs was much concerned with horses. He had usually one or more of his own, as is shown by receipts for payment of Horse Tax, as well as by the bills of a veterinary surgeon [1] ; and in 1799 he paid tax for a cavalry horse which was, probably, for the use of his son. Horses were, of course, necessary if he was to travel in search of orders and to exercise some kind of supervision over his scattered outworkers ; and by 1803, if not earlier, he found it convenient to own his own gig instead of having to hire a carriage whenever he or his family wished to visit friends outside Warrington. (It had leather-covered shafts, was upholstered with canvas, cloth and lace, had a " painted cloth carpet " and was furnished with a sword-case.) But that his interest in horses was more than utilitarian is revealed in several letters from friends such as John Darwin and William Cole, which show that he made a point of being present, whenever business allowed, at the annual race-meetings at Newton, Chester and Manchester. Whether or not he backed horses at the races we do not know. But his bank books and letters show that he occasionally bought a ticket in a lottery— of a firm with the auspicious name of Richardson, Goodluck & Co. And jottings in his handwriting on the back of business letters call up a picture of him, sitting in the evening at the inn, watching his clients playing some now forgotten (and perhaps better forgotten) tavern game, or laying wagers to be paid in ale or punch.[2]

That Stubs was given to hospitality is attested by many letters from those who stayed with him at the *White Bear*. From time to time he would send a cask of ale as a present to his friends in Sheffield, or a Warrington river salmon to Richard Shaw when guests were expected at Daresbury. But his generosity was shown more largely

details see W. Crompton and G. Venn : *The Warrington Volunteers, 1798–1898*, 32.

[1] A bill of 1790 was for treatment of a black horse : another of 1792 makes mention of a grey horse, as well as of a " new horse ". In 1806 Stubs paid tax on two draught horses and one riding horse.

[2] A note on a letter of 27 July, 1790, reads :

Mr. Shuttleworth, Director.	Mr. Shuttleworth, Harlot.
Mr. Jackson, Harlot.	Mr. Mutton, Director.
for 1/– worth of Punch	Mr. Mutton lays 3 pints of Punch to 2.

On the back of another letter of November, 1802, is written :

8–9 width, 6–3 height
Mr. C. betts Mr. B. glasses round
that it is not the above between
stumps.

in his treatment of those in distress. A brother of his wife, Samuel Sutton, seems to have fallen on evil days : for many years he worked as a cobbler and repaired the shoes of the Stubs family [1] ; and another brother-in-law, Thomas Sutton, who had domestic trouble, left his wife, enlisted as a soldier and died. Stubs seems to have looked after the widow of one of these, at least to the extent of paying her rent.[2] And bills from his apothecary, E. Jones, show that he provided medicines at times of sickness not only (as might have been expected) for his apprentices but also for his workmen and their wives.[3]

Young men setting up in business on their own account came to him for help, and were rarely refused. In December, 1796, Edward Smith of Stockport wrote, " I have made another application to my Father for some money which he is not willing to advance on account of my Father in Law not doeing something for me and I know he has none to spare. If you could but help me to 300£ will give you any security I can . . . I now want goods and I can't order for want of paying up my Credit . . . I have no friend else to trust to but yourself and beg you'll doe all you can for me." Again, in March, 1802, the son of Richard Shaw, when sending Stubs £6 in payment of interest, wrote, " I cannot express the obligation I feel myself under to you for your kindness in advanceing me the Money, and your Friendly offers to my Father, when he mentioned to you I was going into the Paper Business." Stubs had not only financed the young man but had also transferred to him part of his orders for wrapping paper. Such warm-heartedness was not always, however, rewarded with thanks : when, in 1799, money was advanced to the son of Thomas Hayter of Tewkesbury, the father wrote reproving Stubs, saying his son had been borrowing of everyone and spending at a very extravagant rate.

That Stubs was a hard worker goes without saying ; and evidence of his enterprising spirit has been given in preceding chapters. File-maker, maltster, brewer, seller of tools, combs and slates, he was always being attracted to some new venture. In 1797 he contemplated buying a retail ironmonger's shop in Manchester ; and Travis & Yates, who wished to sell their business, went so far as to find a young

---

[1] The Stubs family was a large one and the bill for mending shoes from March to November, 1794, came to £9 8s. 6½d. Like most others who worked for Stubs, Sutton was in debt, and £1 19s. was set to Stubs' credit as interest.

[2] The amount was £2 10s. a year and it was payable to C. Rogerson.

[3] A bill of 1795 includes medicine for Cranage, Ridgway's wife, and Boond.

man who was willing to manage it for him as a partner.[1]   In the same
year he considered the purchase of a lot of houses, offered to him by
a J. W. Fisher of Gray's Inn for £550, " before the bill passes, which
is now pending, to lay a duty upon estates sold in private as well
as in public ".   Shortly afterwards he actually bought property of
two young men named Bispham ; and, in later years, demand notes
for Poor Leys suggest that he had come to own one or two small
houses in Warrington.[2]

Possibly the biggest speculation he made was in 1799 when he
became a part-owner in vessels sailing from Liverpool to the Baltic.
He may have been attracted to such an investment by reports of the
large gains which had come to a relative of his, John Stubs of Newton,
from trading and privateering ventures a few years earlier.[3]   But, in
any case, it was natural, in view of his close association with Liverpool,
that he should have embarked part of his capital in foreign trade.
Stubs held one-eighth share in a venture, the other partners in which
were John Barber of Liverpool [4] and Richard Shaw and Thomas
Banner of Daresbury.   The first two of these were timber merchants,
and it is evident that timber was the commodity from the importation
of which profits were sought.   A letter from the captain of one of
the vessels, addressed from Riga Bay on 6 June, 1799, said that the
ship had been aground for thirty hours and had been refloated only
after a great part of the outward-bound cargo of salt had been thrown
overboard ; and the captain mentioned that he was putting in at
Riga to examine the ship's bottom and was then going on to Memel,
" for there is no hopes of timber here ".   In the following year,
either the same or another vessel again left Liverpool for Riga ; and
on 4 October John Barber wrote, " I have no doubt but the hard

[1] The shop was at 108, Market Street Lane.   The young man,
J. Lazenby, had served Travis & Yates in their ironmongery and coffin-
furniture business for three years.   He had since married and set up a
business of his own, but was willing to give this up and manage the
concern for Stubs in return for one-third of the profits.   If necessary,
he said he could put £500 into the business, but in this case, he would
expect a larger share of the profits.

[2] In 1803 he paid 12s. 1d. as poor leys for " Ford's ", £1 12s. 7½d.
for Margaret Gaskell's premises, and £4 7s. for " Mr. Peter Stubb's
Premises what he bought from Peter Chrimes ".   Chrimes, it will be
recalled, was a maltster.

[3] See G. W. Daniels : " The Trading Accounts of a London Merchant in 1794 ", Economic Journal, XXXIII, 517.

[4] The name of John Barber, Timber Merchant, appears in Gore's
Liverpool Directory of 1796 and 1800 : the address is St. James's Street.

blowing weather we have had of late would prove a fair wind for the *Mary Ford* and by this time I hope she is at Riga. So soon as this voyage is performed the acct. shall be settled up to that time, when I have no doubt there will be a very good division to be made upon her."

For a time the enterprise seems to have been successful. On 18 February, 1801, an employee of John Barber wrote as follows :

I am requested by Mr. Barber to inform you that Captn Bell will wait on you at your house tomorrow, with papers respecting the Mary Ford and desires you'll make it convenient to be at home, where Mr. Shaw and Mr. Banner will [be] there to meet you as Mr. B. has wrote to Daresbury to the same effect. I am happy in saying what Mr. Bell will present to you, will give you as well as my friends Messrs. Shaw and Banner great satisfaction, wish you a joyfull meeting and friendly parting.

It seems likely that the *Mary Ford* sailed again immediately, this time, however, with unfortunate results. For five weeks later, on 24 March, Barber wrote concerning claims made in respect of her loss :

Mr. Calrow has given me leave to draw upon him for £1000 on account of the Mary Ford's loss, your proportion £125 for which I now inclose you my draft. I have no doubt but that I shall soon obtain leave to draw again, when you may expect to hear from me again in course. N.B. at present I have not obtained a settlement with the underwriters at Edinburgh but that I expect to take place very soon.

Actually negotiations with the underwriters were protracted. Both hull and cargo had been insured, the latter for £600 upon merchandise valued at £1,200. The underwriters for the hull, however, having admitted total loss of the ship, laid claim to the cargo, which had apparently been saved ; and although in April, 1802, a letter from Barber said that the matter had gone to arbitration, in the following November the dispute was still unsettled. How Stubs came out of it all is not known. But by this time he was busy with the new works he was erecting in Warrington, and henceforth his savings appear to have gone into the less speculative channels of his own trade.

It is to be regretted that there is no single document which might enable us to trace the changes of Stubs' personal fortunes over the years. But demand notes for the payment of taxes throw some little light on these. In 1789 his taxes for the half-year came to 13s. 0¾d., in 1794 to £1 7s. 5½d., in 1799 to £2 9s. 3¾d. and in March, 1806, (exclusive of Income Tax) to £13 8s. 7½d. Since between 1789 and 1806 several changes were made both in the bases of taxation and in assessments these gross figures, of themselves, tell us little or nothing.[1] But inspection of individual items brings out one or two points of interest. Under the Land Tax Stubs paid for the half-year only ¾d. in 1789, 3¾d. in 1794 and 1799, and 7½d. in 1806. Since this tax was virtually a rent charge, it appears either that his holding of land had doubled between 1799 and 1806, or that, in the latter year, the assessor levied both half-yearly instalments together. Clearly, however, Stubs' ownership of land must always have been very small. In 1789 and 1794 he paid 3s., in 1799 4s., and in 1806, £1, as House Tax : up to 1799 his house was assessed at £12 and in 1806, when he had removed to other premises, at £20. In 1794 and 1799 he paid tax on twelve windows, in 1806 on seventeen.[2] Up to 1799 he paid only on a single horse, but in 1806 he was assessed not only on two draught horses but also on a riding horse.[3] No Dog Tax was levied in the earlier years, but in 1799 and 1806 Stubs paid duty on one dog ; and in 1806, he also paid on three male servants.[4] These details are indicative of growing wealth ; but the fact that, at the very end of his life, Stubs paid no tax on armorial bearings or hair powder suggests that he never achieved the ambition—perhaps he never cherished it—of belonging to the class of fashionable gentry.

In 1798 Pitt introduced, for the first time, what was virtually an Income Tax. We have no record of what Peter Stubs paid under this ; but, by good fortune, we do possess an assessment which shows his position as tax-payer under the Income Tax which was imposed when war broke out anew in 1803. The document is without date, but it must relate to either 1803 or 1804. It reads :

To Mr. Peter Stubs
    By Virtue of an Act passed in the 43d year of his present Majesty's reign for granting a contribution on property, professions, trades, and

---

[1] The " assessed taxes " were increased by 10 per cent. in 1790 ; further additions of 10 per cent. were made in 1796 and again in 1797 ; and under the " triple assessment " of 1798 the amount payable was again substantially increased. For details see E. R. A. Seligman : *The Income Tax*, Ch. I.

[2] Payments of Window Tax for the half-year were 9s. 9d. in 1789, 8s. 9d. in 1794, £1 8s. in 1799 and £3 17s. 6d. in 1806.

[3] For Horse Tax his payments were 5s. in 1789 and 1794, 12s. in 1799 (plus 2s. for a Cavalry horse) and £6 12s. 6d. in 1806.

[4] The Dog Tax was 3s. in 1799 and 5s. in 1806. The amount payable on the three male servants was £1.

offices : your charge is as under, for the year ending the 5th of April

Description of Property	Landlords Duty	Tenants Duty	On Trade or Annual Profits	Total £ s. d.
Buildings	7 3 6	2 12 6	28 14 —	
Do.	— — —	1 6		39 10 2
Land	— 10 8	— 8 —		

This information, supplemented by what has been gleaned from other sources, enables us to make a reasoned surmise as to the economic circumstances of Stubs at this period.   If our calculations are correct, he held land worth £10 or £11 a year, a dwelling-house for which he paid £12 a year,[1] an inn which, with its malt-kilns and so on, had a gross annual value of about 70 guineas, and a file-works, in his own possession, worth about the same annual sum.   His profits from trade, which were estimated on the average of three years, came to £700.[2]

[1] This was the rent paid in 1801 ; in 1806 Stubs paid £20 rent for his house.

[2] The Act of 1803 introduced the principle of taxation at the source : the Landlord's Duty was normally payable by the occupier of the property, who, if he was not himself the owner, was entitled to recover the tax from the owner.   Stubs, as we know, was the occupier of land, valued at £15 a year, on which his file-works stood.   But a Memorandum Book in which he set down his payments for ground rents shows that not until 1805 did he begin to deduct Landlord's Tax (at 15s. a year) from the gross rent payable to Thomas Lyon.   Since there is no mention of the 15s. in this assessment we may assume that it relates to a year earlier than 1805, and that Lyon was paying the tax himself.   The 10s. 8d. paid as Landlord's Duty (at 1s. in the £) and the 8s. paid as Tenant's Duty (at 9d. in the £) must, therefore, relate to other land, of an annual value of £10 13s. 4d. held by Stubs.

The Landlord's Duty of £7 3s. 6d. on buildings, at a rate of 1s. in the £, gives an assessment of £143 10s.   This assessable value, however, was reached by deducting an allowance for repairs, not exceeding 5 per cent., from the gross annual value, which must therefore have been about £152.   The gross annual value of Stubs' dwelling-house at this time was £12, so that of all his business premises must have been £140. The Tenant's Duty was levied on the same property as the Landlord's Duty, but it was not payable in respect of dwelling-houses which yielded no money income to the tenant or in respect of premises of which the occupier was also the owner.   We may, therefore, assume that the £2 12s. 6d. paid by Stubs under this schedule related to his tenancy of the inn and malt-kilns.   At 9d. in the £ this gives an assessable value

It thus appears that Stubs was a man in comfortable circumstances, but not a wealthy man. In comparison with that of other well-known industrialists of this period his rise from conditions of relative poverty had not been spectacular, and, as often happens, it was left to the second generation to raise the family fortunes to conditions of affluence. Perhaps he was of too generous a nature ever to have become really rich ; or perhaps it was that the diversity of his activities impeded rather than aided the growth of his income. If he had lived longer he might, indeed, have risen further in the scale of incomes : as it was, he died when only 49 years of age, at a time when he might well have expected to reap a large harvest from his early efforts and from the co-operation of his sons, some of whom were now of an age to play their part in the business.

There is evidence that, from the autumn of 1801, Stubs was a sick man. Many letters from customers over the following four and a half years express concern for his health [1] ; and, though the nature of the illness does not appear, prescriptions from his physician, Dr. Pemberton, suggest that it was connected with throat or lungs.[2] Visits to Buxton were made from time to time, but the malady was

of £70 and a gross value, therefore, of about 70 guineas. We know, however, that the rent of the inn, in 1801, was 50 guineas, and unless this had been increased, the malt-kilns and other property must, therefore, have had an annual value of 20 guineas. Deducting 70 guineas (£73 10s.) from the £140 we reach a figure of £66 10s. as the annual value of the file manufactory.

The income from trade or annual profits was subject to a deduction of 3 per cent. of the income in respect of each dependent child in excess of two. In 1804 Stubs had 13 children living, but 5 of these were eighteen years old or more, and of the remaining 8 two would not count for allowances. If we are right in assuming that his claim was in respect of 6 children, his gross income from trade would seem to have been exactly £700. The calculation of tax is as follows :

	£
Gross income	700
Allowance for 6 children at 3 per cent. each .	126
Taxable Income . .	574

Tax payable on £574, at 1s. in the £ .   .   £28 14s.

[1] From, for example, Richard Shaw, Oct., 1801 ; Warham, Potts & Smith, Feb., 1802 ; John Eyre, Sept., 1802 ; W. Hare, Feb., 1803 and Sept., 1804.

[2] A prescription dated 28 October, 1801, for some kind of cough mixture included the juice of a lemon, and Stubs, with his passion for keeping records, wrote on it, " Lemons were 6d. each when this Draught was made up."

not to be cured by taking the waters.[1]   On 28 February, 1806, Peter Stubs' life came to an end.[2]

The funeral was conducted with all the circumstantial evidences of grief appropriate, in the early nineteenth century, to the occasion. Expenditure was lavish. The making of the shroud, it is true, cost only 3s. ; but the " upholstered oak coffin and brass engraved plate " provided by T. & J. Atherton cost 4½ guineas. In addition to the hearse, the undertaker, John Litton, provided two coaches, two chaises, a velvet pall, thirteen cloaks and " mute staffs and ornaments ". The distribution of the badges of mourning was extensive : Litton supplied 38 hatbands of " Rich Twill'd Black Sarsnett ",[3] with " love ribbon " to tie them, 18 others of " Italian crape ",[4] 43 pairs of men's silk gloves [5] and 31 pairs of ladies' long silk gloves.[6] Altogether, the account came to nearly £80, and this was exclusive of other bills for black clothes for the family and crêpe caps and bonnets for the servants. The tombstone in the Parish Churchyard at Warrington records simply :

PETER STUBS, DIED FEBRUARY
28th 1806. AGED 49 YEARS.

By his Will, dated 13 September, 1801, Stubs left all his real and personal estate to his wife, his son John, his son-in-law William Whitley and Thomas Lee, merchant of Warrington, in trust.[7] They were to pay an annuity of £150 to the widow, Mary Stubs, and a legacy of £200 to each child [8] on reaching the age of 21, or (in the case

---

[1] In 1804 W. Hare of Newark wrote, " I expect Mr. Stubs is for Buxton this summer. I shd. very much like to see him at Harrigate were myself, Wife and Daughter is going " ; and in September he wrote, " I hope Mr. Stubs found benefit from Buxton waters."

[2] His later years must have been clouded by the loss of friends.   In 1801 or early in 1802 John Harrison of Sheffield died, and in 1803 Richard Shaw of Daresbury died at the age of 46.   For the second of these see *Billinge's Liverpool Advertiser*, 4 July, 1803.

[3] " 85½ yd Rich Twill'd Black Sarsnett for 38 Hatbands @ 7/-, £29 – 18 – 6."

[4] At a cost of £3 17s. 6d.

[5] They cost, at 5s. 4d. a pair, £11 9s. 4d.

[6] 31 pairs, at 7s. 9d. a pair, cost £12 0s. 3d.

[7] The terms of the will are recited in a document concerning the Assignment and Release of the Stock in Trade, etc., of the file business, dated 30 January, 1824, in the custody of Messrs. Henry Greenall & Co., Solicitors, Warrington.

[8] Except Sarah, who had already received £200 on her marriage to William Whitley of Ashton-in-Makerfield.

of daughters who might marry before that age) on marriage ; and they were to carry on the business of file-making for 14 years and for so many years thereafter as they should deem fit. John Stubs was to be in charge of the business, under the superintendence of the other trustees, and was to be allowed a salary of £150 a year. Finally, subject to these provisions, the whole of the estate, effects and profits of the business were to be distributed among the children " share and share alike ". It seems to have been a fair disposition.

II

Of Mary Stubs, the wife of Peter, there is little to say. Born on 5 October, 1758, the daughter of Thomas Sutton of Warrington, she was married to Peter Stubs by licence at Warrington Parish Church on 6 July, 1777. Hers was a lot not uncommon to married women of her day. Her first baby was born in the following January ; by 1789 she was already the mother of seven children [1] ; and during the succeeding fourteen years ten more were added to the family.[2] In a bill from Peter Jackson, evidently a surgeon, beginning July, 1791, but not presented for payment until January, 1796, the item " Attending Mrs. Stubbs £1-1s-0d ", occurs five times in four and a half years. Preoccupation with the bearing and rearing of children cannot have allowed of many other activities ; but, as has been seen, Mary Stubs helped her husband in the early years by taking in lodgers, and it seems likely that, later on, she took a share in the management of the *White Bear*. Whether or not travellers stayed at the inn does not appear, but there was much to do in " putting up beds ", stuffing mattresses, making ticks, mending carpets, hanging curtains and so on ; and the bills of one, Ann Rowlinson, who was employed in this work, were usually sent in to Mrs. Stubs.[3] The fact that it was fabric, and not dresses, that she bought of the Warrington drapers shows that she probably made her own clothes and those of her daughters, and orders of chintz for furniture suggest that she did her own upholstery

[1] Sarah, b. 6 Jan., 1778 ; John, b. 1 Dec., 1779 ; Mary, b. 8 Jan., 1782 ; Peter, b. 30 Jan., 1784 ; Thomas, b. 1 Jan., 1786 ; James, b. 2 Apr., 1788 ; William, b. 3 Apr., 1789.

[2] Johnson, b. 1 July, 1791 ; Ellen, b. 30 June, 1792 ; Elizabeth, b. 2 Sept., 1793 ; James, b. 7 Sept., 1794 ; Ann, b. 20 Nov., 1795 ; Joseph, b. 28 Nov., 1796 ; Edward, b. 30 May, 1798 ; Henry, b. 28 May, 1799 ; George, b. 17 June, 1801 ; and Charles, b. 6 Sept., 1803.

[3] Ann Rowlinson was paid 6d. a time for " putting up beds ". She supplied blue or brown paper (at 10d. a quire) to put at the head of the beds, and also feathers and flocks.

too. But in later years, when the family resources were larger, she sometimes indulged in the luxury of having her hair attended to professionally—at a cost of 3*d.* a time for dressing and 6*d.* for cutting. In April, 1794, she obtained the help of a maid-servant, Nanny Richardson; in the autumn of the same year, when her eleventh child was born, her infant daughter, Elizabeth, and the new baby, James, were put out to nurse; and the same practice was followed with succeeding babies. From time to time the nurse, Deborah Taylor, received payments for board of the children, accompanied by loans; and, like nearly all other servants of Stubs, she seems to have been in a condition of chronic indebtedness to her employer.[1]

Bills dated 1789 show that, in that year, the older children were at school in Warrington : Sarah who was then eleven, and John who was nine, were receiving instruction from the Rev. J. Glazebrook ; and Peter, who was not quite six years of age, was under the care of one W. Hume. Mr. Glazebrook charged 2 guineas a year for teaching each child Latin and English, with the addition of 16*s.* for instruction in writing : his bill also included the cost of four sittings in St. James' Church (at 6*s.* each). The fee of W. Hume for teaching Peter for the three months ended 31 December, 1789, was only 4*s.* ; but 2*s.* for a Testament and 1*s.* for " firemoney ", brought the total cost to 7*s.* Two years later, in 1791, Peter and Thomas had joined their brother and sister at Mr. Glazebrook's school ; and the bill for the year (which covered four quarters for John, three for Sarah, and one for Peter and Thomas) came to £7 16*s.* 11*d.*, partly offsetting which, however, was a claim against the reverend schoolmaster of £4 17*s.* for beer and ale. By 1793 John was being taught Accounts, as well as Latin, and Peter was receiving instruction in Elocution. In due course other children—Mary, Thomas and William—were also sent to Mr. Glazebrook, each at a fee of 2 guineas, and the bill for the

---

[1] Several entries at the back of the Malt Book, 1794–7, relate to Deborah Taylor, among them the following :

1795   " Jan. 5. Settled with Deborah for Betty's Board this day and at the same time lent her 10/–. Settled for James & Betty's board up to June 29. Settled for the Children's Board up to July 27 and at the same time lent her two pounds four shillings and she further owes 9/–."

1797   " Settled with Nurse Taylor for son Joseph's Board up to the 24 July. At same time lent her one Guinea."

      " Settled Sep. 11, 1797 for Ann's Board at same time lent her 1–10–0."

1799   " Settled with Deborah for the Children's Board up to April 1, 1799 at same time lent her £4–4–0."

year 1795 (which again was met partly in ale) came to £12 17s. Items on the accounts of the schoolmaster, and others on those of J. Eyres, the Warrington bookseller, show that in these years the children were making use of such books as *Exercises in False English*, and were also improving their minds by reading *The Pilgrim's Progress, Don Quixote, The Hermit, Sperman's Voyages, A History of Prince Lee*, and *The Whole Duty of Man*.

In September, 1793, it was arranged that John should go to board with Peter Stubs' friends, the Coles, and attend as a day-boy the school of a Mr. Stolterforth at Chester ; and during his stay there he sent home the following letters, which throw some light on the progress of his studies.

CHESTER   22 Septr 1793.

DEAR FATHER & MOTHER,

I was much surprized that I did not receive my box yesterday am afraid my mother is worse as she did not send it, it put Miss Cole to great trouble for I had not a clean shirt & she was oblig'd to get one wash'd for me on yesterday afternoon. I hope you will not omit sending it tomorrow. Miss Cole's Compliments to both of you my duty to both of you & love to all my brothers & Sisters not forgetting little Ellen & Betsey as Sarah calls her & am Dear Father & mother
Your dutifull Son
J. STUBS.

N.B. We hear Miles is come to Warrington pray is it true.

P.S. I have begun book keeping.

CHESTER   Octr 27 1793.

HONOR'D PARENTS,

I take this opportunity of writing to let you know I have a shirt missing & would be oblig'd to you to ask my Aunt if she as got it.   On Friday was the Mayor chusing and to day the went to Warbus church with music and the whole Corporation then the 4 Regt. of Royal Irish Dragoons following them and a very pretty sight it was.   My love to all my Brothers & Sisters & to Peter tell him a letter will come as soon without putting speed on it as with, should be glad to hear from you & to hear you grant me my request as in my last.   I am
Honor'd parents,
Your dutiful Son
J. STUBS.

Please to excuse haste as it is almost time to shut up the post office.

CHESTER   Novr 20th 1793.

HONOR'D PARENTS,

I take this opportunity of writing to let you know my Quarter is up on the 18th of Decr. & shou'd be glad to [know] whether I must come home on the 19th because if you wou'd not have [me] to go to that

K

School any longer I had better not to enter on a fresh Quarter so please to let me know in your next. I have not begun Mensuration as yet but shall as soon as Mr. Stolterfoth can get me a case of Instruments, please to send me a bit of blue to mend my coat I have not much to say at present but that Miss Cole is very poorly but hope she be better in the Morning, desires to be remember'd to you & my Aunts family. My love to Brothers & Sisters & hope you will accept the same yourselves.

I am

Honor'd Parents,

Your dutiful Son,

J. STUBS.

The boy remained at Mr. Stolterforth's school for only one term.[1] At the beginning of 1794 he was transferred to Newton, where he stayed as a boarder in a school kept by a Mr. Wallworth, who charged 18 guineas a year for board and 2 guineas a year for instruction. For the seven months ended 29 September, 1794, the bill, including the cost of copybook, quills, ink, paper, washing and the mending of shoes and clothes came to £13 19s. 1d. Two letters, written in April, show that John (at this time fourteen years of age) was trying to collect bills due to his father from a customer in Haydock; they reveal his growing business sense and a gravity of disposition almost out of keeping with his years. Another letter, written from Mr. Wallworth's school, reads as follows :

NEWTON, *July* 4. 1794.

HONOR'D PARENTS,

I receiv'd a Shirt yesterday but I think I have a pair of blue Stockings you have not sent which I would thank you to send with my small tooth comb and a case for my other comb and a black lead pencel for I had the misfortune to loose my case of Instruments and black lead pencil out of my pockett when I came to Newton but I have found my Instruments again. Should be glad to know when the Bishop comes to Warrington as I am at an age to be confirm'd. Mr. Wallworth has given us leave to keep Rabbits & I shou'd be oblige to you if you will send a hung lock and key and staple there is in my brother Peter's drawer & my watch by the bearer. I am

Honor'd Parents

Your dutiful Son

J. STUBS.

The period at Mr. Wallworth's school cannot have been a long one ;

---

[1] The bill for teaching came to £2 2s. 3d., and that of the Cole's for board and washing (which was paid in part by malt and files) to £5 8s. 6d.

for in the following year John was back at Warrington for two quarters' tuition from Rev. J. Glazebrook in English, Writing and Accounts ; and after this, for at least a year he was under a Mr. De la Bove, who charged 2 guineas for " six months' instruction in the French tongue ". Such studies, however, did not occupy the whole of his time. A letter of November, 1795, shows that he was then at Stoke at Mr. Kenwright's house, buying barley for his father—" I shall not part with the money till the barley is ship'd ", he wrote—and from this time onward he was busy travelling in search of orders for files and helping Peter Stubs in other ways.

At the beginning of 1796 Stubs arranged for his sons Peter and Thomas (aged 12 and 10 respectively) to leave Mr. Glazebrook and go with their cousins, the Johnsons, to a school kept by a Richard Willett at Hawarden [1] ; and a little later they were joined there by their brother, William. The fees, covering board and tuition for the year, were 18 guineas for each boy, with additions for books, writing materials and such services as those of the doctor, shoemaker and tailor. The following letters, in all of which the voice is that of young Peter, give some indication of the life and pastimes of the boys at Hawarden.

HAWARDEN, *April 5th* 1796.
HONOR'D PARENTS,

We have not yet received our things and [you] have no need to expect we know were they are. We yet want some Tops and string to spin them with, and a few marbles and also my Brother John's Pilgrims Progress, Sparmans Voyages and a Voyage to the Cape of good Hope and my Sister Mary's Speaker and her Fables and my Ovid and any other books beside you please for me and my Brothers to read at a night for we are quite lost for something to do at a night, and also a tooth brush and tell Mr. Bratt to send Robert some tops and marbles and some little books. We want a school box for that as we have is too little, so you may send them in it and you must be sure send us word to what Inn in Chester they will come to. And also send us word when my Mother will come but would rather she would come to Chester races and then we might go and see one days race and return again. Please to tell my Sister Mary and Sarah and my Brother John to write and send it along with our Parcel. The fever is very ripe about half a mile of us but if it worsens any I will let you know.

So no more but give our love to Father and Mother Brothers and

---

[1] In a reply to Stubs' inquiries, dated 29 January, 1796, Richard Willett wrote, " I have four Vacancies which make up my Complement, and which I will preserve for you and make no Doubt of rendering both you and your Relation entire satisfaction."

Sisters, and also W^m & Easter and hope they are all well as we are at present and am Honor^d Parents

Your dutiful Son
PETER STUBS.

N.B.   Be sure to write by return of Post.

HAWARDEN   *February* 19*th* 1797.

DEAR FATHER,

Mr. Willett desires me to write to You to ask You if it is your Will that any of us should learn to dance as the dancing Master will attend on the 25th of March if He can get a sufficient Quantity to make it worth his while to attend.   The Terms are half a Guinea Entrance and 15s per Quarter but he charges Nothing Entrance to those who have been to a dancing School before and I should be glad if You would answer this Letter as soon as ever you can make it convenient.   Sorry am I to inform You that Mr. Willett has sent his Man to Day to Liverpool to Mr. Sherwood's to inform them of his Son being at the Brink of ~~Posterity~~ Eternity.   He was just got well of the Fever and some other Disorder took him which I doubt will be his End.   So no more from

Your's &c &c
PETER STUBS.

HAWARDEN   *May* 8*th* 1797.

HON^D PARENTS,

We only received our Parcel on Wednesday last or should have certainly returned you our grateful Thanks for it before now and are very much obliged to you for it now.   We three and P. Johnson went to Chester on Thursday and returned yesterday, Mr. Cole's being unwell the Beginning of the Week prohibited our going before.   I hope you will be sure to let us know how poor James Lion goes on in your next and give our best Respects to him if alive and tell him we are very sorry for him.   We have writ & writ to know when our Mother comes and are no wiser yet but I hope you *will either say Yes or No in your next*.   We take it very unkind of you not letting us know of our Sister's Neck being broke or Mary's coming from School or anything.   We are like so many lost Sheep ignorant of every thing that passes.   All our Eyes are well.   Love to yourselves, Brothers and Sisters, E. & W. H. and are

Your ever dutiful Sons,
P. T. & W. STUBS.

N B.   An Answer by return of Post.

(The sister whose neck had been injured was Sarah.   Reference to the misfortune is made in a letter from William Cole on 30 April, 1797. The accident had not, apparently, any long-lasting effects.)

HAWARDEN *May 21st* 1797.

DEAR FATHER,

A Fortnight has now expired. The Vacation begins to draw near. Mr. Cole proposed that We should be at Chester the Morning We break up and breakfast with him and he will have a Chaise ready for Us to go to Preston Brook &c. We had a Letter from our Sister yesterday and She was very well but I suppose you know that better than Us. I beg you will inform Us in your next whether You approve of the above Plan or no, very soon. Pr Johnson, Self & Brothers are to go to Hollywell, this day Fortnight. We are all well and hearty and join in Love to Yourself and Mother, Brothers & Sisters and are Dear Father,

> Your dutiful Sons
> P. T. & W. Stubbs.
> God save
> the King   Amen
> *so be it.*

For whatever reason, William was withdrawn from Mr. Willett's school in the summer and sent to be taught English, Latin and Writing by a J. Woodrow, presumably in Warrington. The bill for tuition for the six months ended Christmas 1797 was only £1 9s., and books (including the *Pleasing Instructor* and *Delectus Sententiarum*) brought the total cost to no more than £2 8s. 7d. Peter and Thomas remained at Hawarden for several years : in July, 1800, Mr. Willett reported that they were well and added that he hoped " to complete Thos in useful Figures, without retarding his Progress in his Books ". By 1801, after Peter had left school, the charge for Thomas had been raised from 18 to 20 guineas a year, and in addition there was a fee of 1 guinea for Dancing. William, it would seem, did not go back to Hawarden. In 1803, when he was fourteen years of age, he was at the school of a John Willan of Weaverham, who charged as much as 15 guineas for the half-year. The curriculum appears to have been similar to that at Hawarden : it included Latin and Rhetoric, and the bill shows an item of " 5s – od, 20 weeks allowance ", for spending money.

As, one by one, the boys left school it was necessary to find them employment. John, as we have already seen, was taken into his father's business, and it was he, perhaps, who was largely responsible for the quickened development of its dealings perceptible in the last years of Peter Stubs' life. Occasional letters, written when on journeys for the firm, exhibit him as a shrewd, hard-headed man of affairs, lacking (though we may do him injustice here) some of the generosity and tolerance that tempered these qualities in his father. It was on his initiative that the making of pins was begun about 1814, and that a large overseas trade in files and other tools was built up through agencies abroad. He died, at the early age of 37, in 1817.

His younger brother, Peter, was of a different mould. In 1798, when the boy had reached the age of fourteen, his father looked about for a concern to which to apprentice him ; and, after negotiations with merchants in Lancaster and Liverpool, on 1 June, 1799, Peter was bound to Hannay & Logan, brokers of Liverpool, for a period of four years. A clause in the indenture prohibited his buying or selling on his own account without the consent of his masters ; but this consent seems to have been given, for within a few months Peter was dealing in such diverse commodities as barrel-hoops, beesoms, mats, soap, butter, gum and ebony. His seems to have been a sanguine, even careless disposition, and his letters suggest a chronic want of money.[1] An unpaid bill for the carriage of four casks of ale, dated 16 November, 1808, gives the information that " Mr. P. Stubs is now in America—his brother Thomas Stubbs says his mother will pay the carriage immediately on application to her in Warrington ". Peter seems to have spent most of the rest of his life abroad : after some years of business on his own account, he obtained a poorly paid post as cashier in a bank in New Brunswick and he died there in October, 1840.

A word or so may be said of the later careers of two other sons of Peter Stubs. When William completed his schooling he joined his brother John in the family concern, and, some years later, his younger brother, Joseph, was also brought into the partnership. It was under the direction of William and Joseph Stubs that the firm acquired premises in Rotherham for the making of the steel used in the file-works at Warrington ; and it is to their credit that in the early 'thirties they gave up, for humanitarian reasons, the manufacture of pins.[2]

---

[1] In October, 1802, when he had supplied his brother, John, with goods for which he had not yet been paid, he wrote, " John, I'm to windward off you, where's your Bill for £12 – 12 ! ! ! ! My Nose is better, much better, thank heaven, how's yours ? Can it smell a 12 Guinea Bill, John ? " But the situation was exceptional : that expressed in a letter of April, 1803, was far more usual. " With Loss of Leather but a tolerable pleasant ride of about 3 Hours on Wednesday last I arrived safe. I met with Company on the Road and got pretty lively . . . I am in Want of the Nerve of War, the Bond of Peace & in many Instances the strongest Joy of Love—Money, but as I expect you'll send the Gig on Saturday I expect I can keep out of Jail that long, but if you should not find it convenient to sent it, by all means send me some Money."

[2] See T. S. Ashton : *Economica. loc. cit.*

Their relations with labour seem to have been excellent. In 1840 the employees of the firm in Warrington met and passed a resolution stating that their employers had " invariably acted with the strictest sense of justice, combined with a boundless liberality towards their workmen " and decided to present each of them with a massive silver-gilt cup,[1] with suitable inscriptions, as a token of esteem. At the dinner which followed in the Warrington Town Hall, on 3 April, 1841, when over two hundred workmen attended, the cups were presented by William Howard and Thomas Boond, the two oldest employees of the firm. The speeches, on both sides, contained the usual complimentary platitudes,[2] but one made by Joseph Stubs deserves a record here. He remarked that " it was a happy thing for a man to have a father born before him ", and that when he came into the concern " he found that his father's mode of conducting the business had got a good name ". It was a just, if hardly adequate, tribute to the life-work of Peter Stubs.

So far very little has been said of the education of the daughters. We know nothing of the early schooling of the eldest of these, Sarah, for she was already eleven years of age when the records begin, in 1789. Her later education seems to have been entrusted exclusively to Mr. Glazebrook and did not continue very long : perhaps, as often happens with eldest daughters, she was needed at home to help in the bringing up of the younger children. Nevertheless, Sarah's life was not without variety, and from time to time she went to stay with the Coles at Chester or with one or other of Stubs' friends at Sheffield. A letter she wrote to her parents in 1794 has already been quoted [3] : the one that follows, which was written during the same visit to Sheffield, seems worth reproducing, not only for the indication it

---

[1] They are described in the *Liverpool Times* of 6 April, 1841, as follows : " The cups are precisely alike except in the inscription, one bearing the name of WILLIAM STUBS Esq., and the other JOSEPH STUBS Esq. They were covered by glass shades, and rested on rich crimson velvet cushions. In form they are antique, with handles and covers ; they contain about three quarts each. They are covered with a profusion of shells, scrolls, and flowers. The family arms, an arm and battle-axe, are embossed in high relief, and present a very rich and massive appearance. The weight of each cup is between eighty and ninety ounces, and the value of each about sixty guineas."

[2] A full account of the proceedings is given in a booklet : *An Account of the Dinner and Presentation of Plate to Messrs. W. & J. Stubs by their Workmen*, 1841.

[3] *Supra*, 43.

affords of the stage of literacy reached by Sarah at the age of sixteen, but also for the further glimpse it gives of a very charming young person.

SHEFEILD, *April* 29, 1794.

HON^D PARENTS,

I arrived safe at Shefeild last night and found Mr. Parkins Family very well. We went out to sup last Night and as had company to day. There has a Gentleman dined here to day from London he calls his name Hurst. He enquired very kindly after you he his a File maker he asked if I was your Sister he was quit astonished when I said I was your Daughter. Mr. Perkins came to meet me yesterday and I am going their to day. Mr. and Mrs. Parkin makes very much on me. I donat see anything distressing yet. Mrs. Parkin seems to be a very agreeable good kind of woman. There is good many people that I am got aquainted I can hardly understand they talk so queer. Mr. Alkock gave me a bill for Mr. Harison. I only saw young Mr. Harison and the old woman the old woman did not speak to me she was stood at the entry end in an old stuf gown and an old bonet you would hardly pick up in the street but the young man asked come and stop awhile but I think I would rather chuse to stop where I ham. I was very sick comming in the coach betwixt Manchester and buxton and I doubt you will be as sick as I was when I tell you that I paid 18 for riding. We changed horses 4 times and every time we had to pay a fresh coach man that made it 20, we paid 18 for a very plain dinner indeed as eve I seat down to. I have no more to say at present but will write again after a while.

I am Hon^d Parents
Your dutifull Daughter
SARAH STUBS.

Of the upbringing of the second daughter, Mary, it is possible to give more detail. It seems likely that a bill from a private residential school (probably in or near Warrington), dated 31 December, 1789, and covering the expenses of a " Miss Stubs ", relates to her. The charge for board for six months was 6½ guineas, in addition to which there were fees of 12*s.* for the teaching of " writing and casting ", and £1 14*s.* for " Embroidery, Artificial Flowers, Filigree and hair-work " ; and extras, including 6*d.* for " drawing her bird ", and other payments for candles, quills, pencils, copybooks, dancing and washing, brought the total to £13 15*s.* 6¾*d.* In 1791 the cost of board had risen to 8 guineas for the six months, and drawing, sampler-work and English grammar had been added to the curriculum.

After a short period, when she attended school with her brothers under Mr. Glazebrook, Mary, then in her fourteenth year, went on an extended visit as a paying guest to the Coles in Chester.[1]   Meanwhile, her father was looking for a better school than Warrington could offer for a girl of her age.   On the advice of a friend he made inquiries of a Mrs. Mary Knowles, who kept a school for girls in Rodney Street, Liverpool, and received the following reply :

LIVERPOOL, February 18th 1797.

SIR,

I have rec'd your Letter in which you request me to send you the terms of ye School, they continue the same as they were at the Time of Mrs. Bolton's Daughter being under my Care, who, I find, has done me Favour to recommend the School.   Two young Ladies who have just completed their Education & quitted School, give me an Opportunity of receiving two more.   If you should therefore honour me with the Care of your Daughter's Education, you may depend upon my utmost Endeavours for her Improvement.

I am Sir

Terms 18 Guineas p Annum   Your Hble Servant
Entrance 1 Guinea.   MARY KNOWLES.

The house in which the school was held was probably the one now numbered 14 Rodney Street, and the Mrs. Bolton to whom reference is made in the letter was perhaps the wife of John Bolton, who had previously lived there himself : he had taken a lease of it from the Corporation of Liverpool in 1789, and another parcel of land, leased by him at the same time, went in 1804 to a Richard Knowles.[2]

Judging by present appearances the building cannot have been very satisfactory for the purpose of a school : it had no bathroom and, like most of its neighbours in Rodney Street, probably depended for its water-supply on a surface-well in the basement.   Conditions in the dormitories, it is plain, must have been far from pleasant, and perhaps Mary found things somewhat austere, compared with life at home.   In any case, she showed herself sensitive to a difference

[1] In May, 1796, Peter Stubs paid William Cole 10 guineas to cover her board.

[2] The name of Richard Knowles appears in the Directory of 1781 as that of a schoolmaster in Clifton Street.   In 1791 (as the Directory of that year shows) he had a Commercial Academy in Hood Street ; and in 1796, his name appears as a schoolmaster, both at the Commercial Academy and in Rodney Street at the same address as the Ladies' Boarding School kept by Mrs. Knowles.   It seems very probable, therefore, that the Knowles' were husband and wife.   For these and other facts in the text I am indebted to Professor Veitch.

of status that was at once apparent between herself and some of her fellow pupils, and, with due diffidence, asked if this could be remedied.

LIVERPOOL *March 5th.* 1796.
DEAR PARENTS,

It is with the greatest pleasure I take up my pen to write to you, to inform you I like the Satuation you have had the goodness to place me in, only for one reason which is that all the young Ladies of my Age in the school are Parlour Boarders. I therefore should be much happier if you would have the kindness to let me be one. The Difference the young Ladies tell me is 6 Guineas a year. If you have any objections I will not desire it. I will be obliged to you if you will send me some Towels, as the young Ladies find their own. Inform me if you pease by your next Letter if you paid the Carriage for my Box to Liverpool. give my love to my Brothers and Sisters & accept the same

From your Dutifull Daughter
MARY STUBS.

Whether Peter Stubs rose to the occasion, or not, we have no means of knowing ; but surely a man of his sensibility could not have turned a deaf ear to so delicately worded a petition. When Mary finished her schooling she seems, like her sister, Sarah, to have remained at home, though, in her case also, the domestic routine was tempered by occasional holidays with friends. A letter from her, written in December, 1800, suggests that she found less excitement in a visit to Sheffield than her sister had done, and a hint of something like home-sickness is to be detected between the lines.

DEAR PARENTS,

Mr. Hall call'd on me last week. I was happy to hear you were all well and got the Fair over without much trouble. Mr. Smith is expected home on Wednesday. Miss Sarah Eyre returns with me on Saturday, but Mr. Eyre says I shall not go than you write for me. I am not of so much consequence as I think of or you could not have spared me so long. I am afraid we shall not have a pleasant journey home, the Snow is seven yards deep on the Moores, the Coach does but go twice a week now on Mondays and Fridays.

Mr. Eyres and Mr. Smiths Familys make their best respects to you and Sister Whiteley, give my love to Brothers and Sisters my Duty to my Mother and accept the same

from your dutiful Daughter
MARY STUBS.

By this time two younger girls, Ellen (born June, 1792) and Elizabeth (born September, 1793) had come of school age. They were being taught writing and grammar by a W. Birtch, in 1802 at a fee of 8s. 6d. a quarter, and in 1803 (when, however, they attended school only half-days) at 5s. a quarter. At the same time other younger children were receiving education at the hands of A. Allard and A. Male, whose bill addressed to Mrs. Stubs on 29 September, 1803, was for " one Quarter Instruction for five at 6s. . . . £1–10s–0d ". How there came to be five is not clear ; for although, apart from those of whom an account has already been given, there were still five small children in the family (Joseph, Ann, Edward, George and Charles) the last two of these, born respectively in 1801 and 1803, were obviously too young for formal lessons. Is it possible that Mrs. Stubs, not satisfied with her own brood of thirteen, was taking responsibility for the education of the children of some other mother ? A bill sent to her by W. Birtch for " School wages for Alice Atherton " in 1809 shows that the conjecture is not fantastic.

By 1805 Ellen and Elizabeth were old enough to leave Mr. Birtch and go to a school kept by a Martha Cochran at Wigan. The fees here were a good deal higher than those paid for their older sisters at an earlier period : they came to 14 guineas each for a half-year ; and additional charges brought the total cost of education for the two girls to £52 17s. 10d. for the first half-year and £48 15s. for the second.[1] In acknowledging payment of her account in August, 1805, Martha Cochran gave a satisfactory report : " I am happy to add the young ladies are well and in good spirits, and that they have been very good girls during their residence in my family." [2]

Enough has been said—perhaps more than enough—to show that Peter and Mary Stubs did their duty by their numerous children. The feature of interest to the social historian is the low cost of a polite education (including board) at a time when school-masters and mistresses had to rely entirely on fees for their income. Even at the prices of the eighteenth century, to have kept a growing child and given efficient teaching for 18 guineas a year (or, for that matter, half a year) must have meant close economy and a humble standard of comfort for both teacher and pupil.

To pursue further the history of either the Stubs family or the

---

[1] Apart from fees for Dancing and Drawing the " extras " included such items as a box of colours (12s.), use of the harpsichord (5s.), a seat in church (2s. 6d.), a ticket for the Play (3s.), and pocket-money (3s. 6d.). Another bill for the first half of 1806 mentions a foot-stool (9s.), flower-baskets (6s. 6d.), and note-cases (3s. 6d.), for Betsey—all of them probably objects for embroidery.

[2] They remained at Wigan till the summer of 1806. Bills paid to a writing master, John Howard, in the later months of the year and in 1807 suggest that by this time they were back in Warrington.

business itself would be to overstep limits of time which have been respected in previous chapters : the story must be left to some future student, who, if he tells it with the details the records allow, will write a far longer book than this. Suffice it here simply to say that a descendant of Peter Stubs is still connected with the concern, that the *P.S.* files have a high reputation with mechanics to-day, not only in England but also in other parts of the world, and that some of those who make them bear the names of men who have figured in these pages.

Complaint is often made that economic historians leave the minds of their readers cloyed with facts and empty of generalizations. If the charge is made against the present writer his defence must be that it would be hazardous in the extreme to try to induce generalizations from the records of a single firm. What has been attempted is simply to select from a heap of discrete facts those which seemed of chief significance, to piece these into a crude mosaic, and so to offer a picture of a small section of English industrial society at a particular point of time. It was a point of time at which, elsewhere, momentous changes were being made in the technique and structure of manufacture. A few miles away, across the plains to the east of Warrington, a rush of invention was transforming the textile trades, sweeping away the acquired skill of domestic workers, and substituting new methods based on steam-driven machinery. In the tool-making trades, where the application of machine-processes was less easy, there was no such industrial revolution : here changes came slowly, the result of a progressive widening of the market and a need for greater accuracy of workmanship.

The Stubs records illustrate the gradual nature of the transformation that was taking place. For the employer, the years covered by this study were a period of transition (in the words of Mr. Fay) " from indirect mercantile control to direct industrial employment ". Peter Stubs, the inn-keeper, who gave out work to scattered domestic craftsmen, was in process of becoming the modern type of employer, hiring labour to work in a factory owned by himself. He has been seen reaching from near to more distant markets for his raw materials, building up a goodwill, extending his sales to widely scattered customers, making use of newly specialized agencies of transport and finance, seeking fresh outlets for his accumulated profits, and laying the foundation of a family fortune. For the workers, also, it was a period of transition—transition from the dubious independence of the workshop attached to the home, with all the anxieties associated with under-employment and debt, to the closer dependence and rigid hours of the factory, with, however, the assurance of some regularity of work and the payment of weekly wages in cash. It is no business of ours to decide whether, for either employer or workers, the former or the latter state was the more eligible. Our concern has been simply to trace the course of events. Only when we have many more such studies than have yet been made will it be possible to speak with confidence about—let alone pass judgment on—those spontaneous forces of social development which it is the ultimate aim of the economic historian to discover and understand.

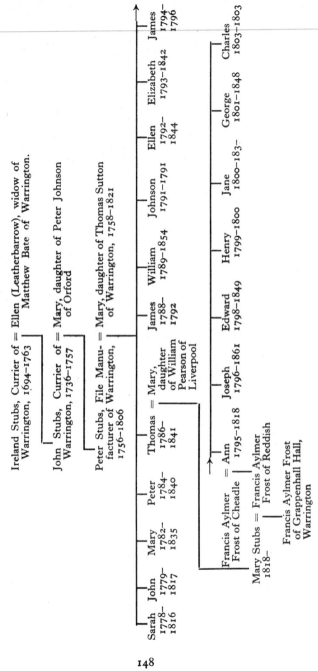

THE FAMILY OF STUBS

Ireland Stubs, Currier of = Ellen (Leatherbarrow), widow of
Warrington, 1694–1763   Matthew Bate of Warrington.

John Stubs, Currier of = Mary, daughter of Peter Johnson
Warrington, 1736–1757   of Orford

Peter Stubs, File Manu- = Mary, daughter of Thomas Sutton
facturer of Warrington,   of Warrington, 1758–1821
1756–1806

Sarah   John   Mary   Peter   Thomas = Mary,   James   William   Johnson   Ellen   Elizabeth   James
1778–   1779–   1782–   1784–   1786–   daughter   1788–   1789–1854   1791–1791   1792–   1793–1842   1794–
1816   1817   1835   1840   1841   of William 1792   1844   1796
                                                          Pearson of
                                                          Liverpool

Francis Aylmer = Ann   Joseph   Edward   Henry   Jane   George   Charles
Frost of Cheadle 1795–1818   1796–1861 1798–1849 1799–1800 1800–183– 1801–1848 1803–1803

Mary Stubs = Francis Aylmer
1818–   Frost of Reddish

Francis Aylmer Frost
of Grappenhall Hall,
Warrington

148

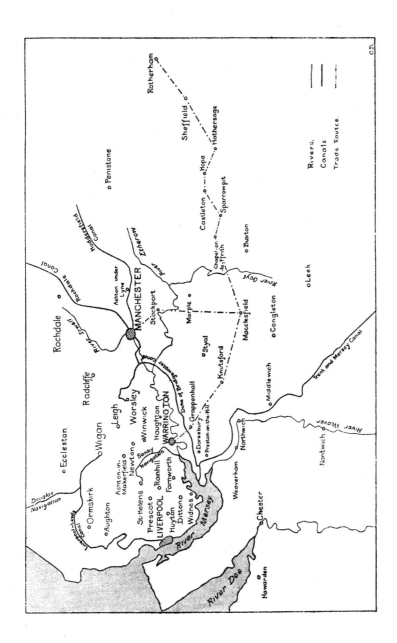

INDEX

L

Printed by offset litho in Great Britain by Taylor Garnett Evans & Co, Ltd
Watford, Hertfordshire